THE TASTE OF OUR TIME

Collection planned and directed by

ALBERT SKIRA

BIOGRAPHICAL AND CRITICAL STUDY

BY

PIERRE ROSENBERG

Translated from the French by Helga Harrison

CHARDIN

SKIRA

Title page:
The Brioche, also called A Dessert (detail), 1763. Louvre, Paris.

★

© 1963 by Editions d'Art Albert Skira.
Library of Congress Catalog Card Number: 63-20241.

★

Distributed in the United States by
THE WORLD PUBLISHING COMPANY
2231 West 110th Street, Cleveland 2, Ohio

"...these accomplished works in which not a single brushstroke is isolated, wherein each part draws its *raison d'être* from the others, and imposes its own upon them."

MARCEL PROUST

EIGHTEENTH-CENTURY French art has lost its appeal. Boucher, Fragonard, and Hubert Robert still retain a certain charm, but few would claim for them a place among the masters who have added luster to the history of art. Chardin himself is no longer revered as once he was. His "modest distinction" and his "magic" have ceased, if not to touch us, at least to charm us. For some two hundred years the same sort of clichés and the same sort of adjectives have been used about him. It is true that his pictures fetch sensational prices at the big sales; it is true too that nobody dares to criticize him—quite the contrary, in fact— but his work no longer inspires affection. The disrepute into which the eighteenth century has fallen has somewhat tarnished his reputation, despite a revival of interest in the still life.

What are the things usually said about Chardin? A bourgeois painter, a member of the Parisian lower middle-classes, so much a part of Paris that he would never leave it. In this he is a contrast to Fragonard, the companion of royal mistresses. Though not hard-working himself, he celebrates the industrious virtues of his class—honest, robust, open, but despised—on the eve of the Revolution.

To this image, which is beginning to date, our own century has preferred another—that of the lucid architect of paintings whose subjects are no more than a pretext for cunning feats of composition. This is the image vigorously put forward by the Cubists, who count him as one of their masters.

Neither of these images can be called a false one. Each expresses the truth of an age. But when we consider the instinctive perfection of his work, its social significance and the technical principles that underlie it seem unimportant.

This book does not claim to rediscover Chardin. Still less does it claim to put forward new facts and dates or new attributions, or even to suggest a chronology of his work. In fact, chronology has been deliberately disregarded in the arrangement of the illustrations which pass from small domestic scenes to still lifes, and from half-length portraits to pastels. It may be considered reprehensible, to say the least of it, to ignore the evolution of a style, the slow development of a life's work, in this way. But is there really any evolution? Can we speak of Chardin's having made his career, in the sense that Poussin and Picasso made theirs, building it up in the same way as they composed one of their pictures? Has each of Chardin's works an immutable place and do we threaten the stability of the whole if we place it differently? We do not think so. The illustrations are thus intended not so much to show any chronological development as to evoke the various sides of the painter's personality. This arrangement has made it possible for us to accompany the selected texts from Diderot to Francis Ponge, at the end of the book, with reproductions of certain representative masterpieces varying in style and widely separated in date. Each of these works is a kind of tribute: *The Skate*, to Matisse, who was to copy it; the *Self-Portrait* to Cézanne, who admired it; the *Attributes of Music* to the Cubists, who were to make full use of subject and composition alike; the *Clay Pipe and Earthenware Jug* to Braque.

All we ask is that the reader should pause for a moment in front of each of the artist's paintings: pause in the same casual way as the figures in these paintings, caught in mid-gesture as they go quietly about their everyday tasks.

6

CHRONOLOGICAL SURVEY

1699 November 2. Birth in Paris, Rue de Seine, of Jean Siméon Chardin, son of Jean Chardin and Jeanne Françoise David, his second wife. The official records give his name as Jean Siméon, not Jean-Baptiste Siméon. He was baptized the next day at the church of Saint-Sulpice.

Chardin was born two years after the Peace of Ryswick, high-water mark of the reign of Louis XIV, nine years after the death of Lebrun, four years after that of Mignard and La Fontaine. Watteau was his elder by fifteen years, Voltaire by five years, G. B. Tiepolo by three years, Canaletto and Hogarth by two years. The first two decades of the century saw the birth of the following artists and writers: Longhi (1702), Boucher (1703), Maurice Quentin de La Tour (1704), Goldoni (1707), Pompeo Batoni (1708), Guardi and Jean-Jacques Rousseau (1712), Diderot (1713), Pigalle and Gluck (1714), C. N. Cochin the Younger (1715), E. M. Falconet (1716), d'Alembert (1717), Piranesi (1720).

1699 Birth of Subleyras and Jussieu.
Publication of Fénelon's "Aventures de Télémaque."

1700 Philip of Anjou becomes King of Spain, reigning as Philip V.

1706 Birth of Benjamin Franklin.

1709 The French beaten by Marlborough at the Battle of Malplaquet.

1713 Peace of Utrecht. Controversy over the papal bull "Unigenitus."

1715 Death of Louis XIV. Le Sage begins the publication of "Gil Blas."

1715-1723 Regency of Philip, Duke of Orleans, during the minority of Louis XV.

1716 Death of Leibnitz. The Venetian painters Sebastiano and Marco Ricci pass through Paris.

1717 Death of Jean Jouvenet. Watteau presents his "Embarcation for Cythera" (Louvre) to the Academy as his reception piece.

1718-1728 Chardin studies under Pierre-Jacques Cazes, then under Noël-Nicolas Coypel.

1719-1720 Publication of "Robinson Crusoe."

Before 1720 The Chardins move to a house at the corner of Rue Princesse and Rue du Four.

1720 Watteau's "Enseigne de Gersaint" (Berlin).

1720-1721 G. A. Pellegrini, visiting Paris with his sister-in-law Rosalba Carriera, decorates the ceiling (now destroyed) of the gallery in the Banque Royale, now Banque de France. Financial crisis in France following the collapse of John Law's "Mississippi scheme."

1721 Death of Watteau. Montesquieu's "Lettres Persanes."

1723 May 6. Marriage contract between Chardin and Marguerite Saintard, who comes of a well-to-do family.

1723 Death of the Duke of Orleans and official beginning of the reign of Louis XV. Birth of Sir Joshua Reynolds.

1724 February 3. Chardin enrolled by his father as master-painter at the Academy of St Luke, the craftsmen's guild, whose status was now far inferior to that of the Royal Academy of Painting and Sculpture. Chardin later repudiated his connection with the guild of St Luke. It was about this time that he first attracted attention with the signboard (now lost) that he painted for a surgeon-barber.

1724 Birth of Kant, Gabriel de Saint-Aubin and Henri Horace Roland de La Porte.

1725 Birth of Greuze. Marriage of Louis XV with Marie Leczinska. Death of Peter the Great.

1726 Publication of "Gulliver's Travels."

1727 Birth of Gainsborough and G. D. Tiepolo. Death of Newton.

1728 June 3. Chardin shows several pictures at an exhibition in the Place Dauphine, including "The Skate" (Louvre).
September 25. Nominated to the Royal Academy and admitted the same day as a painter "in the domain of animals and fruit." He presents the Academy with his "Skate" and "Sideboard" (Louvre). Much impressed by Chardin's still lifes, Largillierre played a large part in this rapid success.

1729 February 5. He resigns from the Academy of St Luke, which however prided itself on having numbered him among its members.

1730 December 31. Betrothal with Marguerite Saintard.

1730 Death of François de Troy. Marivaux's "Le Jeu de l'Amour et du Hasard."

1731 January 17. Chardin and Marguerite Saintard revoke their marriage contract of 1723, her family having suffered heavy losses in the meantime, owing no doubt to the collapse of Law's financial schemes.
January 26. New marriage contract, which gives us information as to Chardin's worldly circumstances at the time.
February 1. The marriage takes place at Saint-Sulpice.
November 18. Baptism of Pierre-Jean Chardin, their first-born son. Though an artist of recognized standing, Chardin has difficulty in making ends meet and is obliged to accept any work he can find. Hired as Jean-Baptiste Van Loo's assistant to restore the paintings in the Galerie de François I at Fontainebleau.

1731 Abbé Prévost's "Manon Lescaut."

1732 Exhibits in the Place Dauphine. One of his pictures, representing a bas-relief in bronze by François Flamand, is universally praised and bought by J. B. Van Loo.

1732 Birth of Fragonard, Beaumarchais and Haydn.

1733 Chardin's first figure paintings.
August 3. Baptism of his daughter Marguerite-Agnès (died 1737).

1733 Death of Couperin. Birth of Hubert Robert.

1734 Exhibits sixteen pictures in the Place Dauphine, including the "Lady sealing a Letter" (Berlin), dated 1733.

1734-1753 Publication of Saint-Simon's "Mémoires."

1735 Death of Chardin's wife, April 14. The inventory of her estate, drawn up in 1737, includes a sketch by Watteau.

1735 Rameau's opera "Les Indes Galantes."
1736 The Venetian painter Jacopo Amigoni passes through Paris.

1737 Reopening of the Salon, which had not taken place since 1704 (except for 1725). Chardin exhibits at least eight pictures, notably a "Laundress" (probably the Stockholm version). From now on he exhibits regularly at the Salon, sometimes his latest works, sometimes older pictures.

1737 Death of the sculptor François Lemoyne.

1738 Exhibits nine pictures at the Salon, including the "Child with a Top" (Louvre): the "Draftsman" now in Berlin (dated 1737) and perhaps the Stockholm version as well; also "The Cellar Boy" and "The Scullery Maid" (probably the Glasgow versions, dated 1738). The first print after a picture by Chardin. The Mercure de France refers to his "great reputation."

1739 Six pictures at the Salon, including the "Lady drinking Tea" (Glasgow), dated 1738, and the "Return from Market" (Louvre) dated 1739.

1740 Five pictures at the Salon, among them "Saying Grace" (Louvre). "Naive," "piquant," "natural" and "lifelike" are the terms most frequently applied to his work by the critics of the day.
Presented to Louis XV, Chardin gives the king his "Hardworking Mother" and "Saying Grace" (both now in the Louvre).
C. N. Cochin's first prints after pictures by Chardin.

1740 Frederick the Great becomes King of Prussia and Maria Theresa Empress of Austria. Richardson publishes "Pamela."

1740-1745 Coustou's "Chevaux de Marly," now at the entrance to the Champs-Elysées in Paris.

1741 Two pictures at the Salon: "The Morning Toilet" (Stockholm) and "Girl with a Shuttlecock" (Rothschild Collection).
"The public continues to sing the praises of Monsieur Chardin" (Mercure de France).

1741 Birth of the sculptor J. A. Houdon.

1742 Chardin falls seriously ill and goes through a crisis which marks a turning point in his career. He does not exhibit at the Salon and no paintings can be assigned to this year.

1743 Death of his mother. Exhibits three pictures at the Salon. Appointed "adviser to the Royal Academy of Painting and Sculpture."

1743 Birth of Lavoisier. Death of Vivaldi, Desportes, Lancret and Rigaud.

1744 November 1. Marriage contract between Chardin and Françoise-Marguerite Pouget, a widow aged 37. Among the witnesses are his brother Juste Chardin, "cabinetmaker to the King," and the painter Aved.

November 26. The marriage takes place at the church of Saint-Sulpice and Chardin moves to a house owned by his wife, at 13 Rue Princesse.

1744 Birth of Anne Vallayer-Coster.

1745 October 21. Birth of a daughter, Angélique-Françoise Chardin, who died young. Patronized from now on by some of the most famous collectors of the day, among them Count Tessin, the Prince of Liechtenstein and the King of Sweden.

1745 Le Normand de Tournehem appointed Director General of Royal Buildings. The "reign" of Madame de Pompadour begins. Servandoni finishes the façade of Saint-Sulpice.

1746 Four pictures at the Salon: two genre scenes, "Saying Grace" (a replica) and "Recreations of Private Life," and two portraits.

1746 Death of Largillierre. Birth of Goya.

1747 Exhibits only one picture at the Salon. Fragonard is said to have been Chardin's pupil for a few months about this time.

1747 Death of Francesco Solimena and Giuseppe Maria Crespi.

1748 Again he shows only one picture at the Salon (now held every two years), a "Draftsman sketching M. Pigalle's 'Mercury'." Reproached by the critics for the "rarity" of his works.

1748 Birth of David. Montesquieu's "L'Esprit des Lois."

1749 Death of Magnasco. Fielding's "Tom Jones" and the first volume of Buffon's "Histoire Naturelle." Birth of Goethe.

1750 Death of Bach. Excavations begin at Pompeii.

1751 Exhibits one picture: "Lady with a Bird-Organ" (Frick Collection, New York). A critic takes him to task for his laziness: "With the talent Monsieur Chardin possesses, how pleased his admirers would be, were he as hard-working and prolific as Monsieur Oudry!"

> 1751 Voltaire's "Siècle de Louis XIV" and the first volume of the "Encyclopédie."

1752 Chardin's "Lady with a Bird-Organ" is bought by the king for 1500 francs, the highest price paid for any of his pictures in his lifetime. Granted an annual pension of 500 francs by the Director General of Royal Buildings.

> 1752 Death of Jean-François de Troy the Younger.

1753 Exhibits nine pictures at the Salon, which meet with the highest praise from the critics—this is the zenith of his career.

1754 Thanks to his father's backing, Pierre-Jean Chardin, the artist's son by his first wife, is awarded the Grand Prix of the Academy for a painting on an historical theme.

> 1754 The Marquis de Marigny, Madame de Pompadour's brother, appointed Director General of Royal Buildings. The Place de la Concorde laid out by J. A. Gabriel. Death of G. B. Piazzetta.

1755 Chardin unanimously elected Treasurer of the Academy. For the first time he takes charge of hanging and arranging the pictures exhibited at the Salon, where he himself shows two paintings. Again and again critics compare him with La Fontaine.

> 1755 Birth of Elisabeth Vigée-Lebrun. Death of Jean-Baptiste Oudry.

1756 Shows a renewed interest in still life painting, the first version of the "Makings of a Lunch" (Carcassonne) dating to this year. The "Portrait of Chardin" engraved by Laurent Cars after a drawing by C. N. Cochin is put on sale.

> 1756 Birth of Mozart.

1757 Moves from the Rue Princesse to the Louvre, where he has been granted living quarters by royal warrant. Exhibits six pictures at the Salon, two of them from the collection of La Live de Jully. Dispute between Chardin and his son over the property left by the first Madame Chardin. Pierre-Jean leaves for Rome to study at the Académie de France.

1757 Birth of William Blake. Death of Rosalba Carriera.

1758 Birth of the painter Pierre-Paul Prud'hon.

1759 Exhibits nine pictures at the Salon, including seven still lifes. Reviewing the Salon for the first time, Diderot is far from being enthusiastic over Chardin's work. Pierre-Jean Chardin, now studying at the Académie de France in Rome, is described by the director, Charles Natoire, as "one of the weakest fellows of them all."

1759 Birth of Schiller and Canova. Death of Handel. Voltaire's "Candide" and Sterne's "Tristram Shandy."

1760 La Tour makes a pastel portrait of Chardin, who presents it to the Academy in 1774 (now in the Louvre).
Chardin is known to have been very friendly at this time with a group of artists that included the draftsman Desfriches, the painter Vien and the engraver Wille. He now paints two of his finest still lifes: "The Jar of Olives" (Louvre) and "The Sliced Melon" (one version dated 1760, another in the Louvre).

1761 Already Treasurer of the Academy, Chardin is now officially charged with the exacting and delicate task of hanging the pictures at the Salon. It was Cochin who urged the Marquis de Marigny to appoint him to this position. Almost at once a quarrel breaks out between Chardin and Jacques Oudry over the hanging of the latter's pictures at the 1761 Salon. Chardin himself exhibits eight pictures, including the "Flower Piece" (Edinburgh). "The merits of Monsieur Chardin are universally recognized," writes the art critic of the Mercure de France.

1761 Jean-Jacques Rousseau publishes "La Nouvelle Héloïse" and Greuze paints "L'Accordée de Village."

1762 Chardin is delegated by the Academy to call on Pigalle, who is ill. Works by this sculptor figure in a number of Chardin's pictures.
Pierre-Jean Chardin kidnapped by pirates at Genoa.

1762 Rousseau's "Emile" and "Contrat Social." Diderot writes "Le Neveu de Rameau." Catherine the Great becomes Empress of Russia. Birth of André Chénier.

1762-1764 The Petit Trianon built by J. A. Gabriel.

1763 Cochin solicits the Marquis de Marigny for an increase in the yearly pension paid to Chardin. He exhibits six pictures at the Salon, among them "The Brioche" or "Dessert" and "The Jar of Olives" (both in the Louvre). Diderot is now enthusiastic: "This man is a painter, this man is a colorist . . . There is no way of explaining this magic—these thick layers of color . . ." "The Brioche" (Louvre), one of the masterpieces of his maturity, dates to this year.

1764 Thanks to Cochin, Chardin is given an order for three overdoor panels, "The Attributes of the Arts, Music and Sciences," for the Château de Choisy. Two of these are now in the Louvre, the third is lost. He was paid 800 francs apiece for them.

1764 Death of Madame de Pompadour. Soufflot begins building the Panthéon. Watt's first steam engine.

1765 Presenting himself as a candidate at the instance of Cochin and Descamps, Chardin is elected a member of the Academy of Rouen. He exhibits at least eight pictures at the Salon, including the three overdoor panels for the Château de Choisy and the "Basket of Grapes" (Angers) dated 1764. Diderot again waxes enthusiastic over his work. It is in his review of this Salon that he quotes Chardin at length: "Gentlemen, may we crave your indulgence . . ."

1765-1770 The "Confessions" of Jean-Jacques Rousseau.

1767 He exhibits only two pictures at the Salon: the two overdoor panels ordered in 1766 for the king's Château de Bellevue. Pierre-Jean Chardin, known to have been in Venice at this time, is thought to have committed suicide there a few years later. "His giddy head never made it possible for him to come to any good," wrote Cochin, who spoke of the "grief his father felt at his death, the more so as it looked like suicide." He added: "Few pictures by him remain, for incapable as he was of painting any to his satisfaction, he finished practically none."

1768 At the solicitation of Cochin, Chardin's yearly pension is increased by 300 francs following the death of J. Restout.

1769 Chardin exhibits nine pictures at the Salon. He falls ill several times in the course of the year.

1769 Birth of Sir Thomas Lawrence.

1770 Cochin, hitherto the all-powerful secretary to the Academy, sees his influence diminish with the appointment of Jean-Baptiste Pierre as Director. The latter shows little favor towards Chardin, whose influence is now on the decline. At Boucher's death, however, Cochin succeeds in increasing Chardin's pension by 400 francs.

1770 Death of G. B. Tiepolo. Marriage of the dauphin, the future Louis XVI, with Marie-Antoinette. Birth of Hölderlin, Beethoven and Wordsworth.

1771 Chardin exhibits four pictures at the Salon, including (for the first time) some pastels. He turned to this technique late in life, probably because he found it less fatiguing for his eyes. "This is a genre which he had not yet practised, and which at his first attempt he has carried to the highest pitch," exclaimed the art critic of L'Année Littéraire. The fine "Self-Portrait with Spectacles" (Louvre) dates to this year.

1771 Birth of Sir Walter Scott.

1772 Death of Swedenborg.

1773 He exhibits one painting and one pastel at the Salon. His health is giving way and he is obliged to sell his house in the Rue Princesse.

1773 Diderot writes "Jacques le Fataliste." The Comte d'Angiviller succeeds Marigny as Director General of Royal Buildings.

1774 He resigns his position as Treasurer of the Academy. The task of hanging the pictures at the Salon is entrusted to Vien, while Coustou succeeds Chardin as Treasurer.

1774 Death of Louis XV and accession of Louis XVI. Goethe publishes "Die Leiden des Jungen Werthers."

1775 The new Director General of Royal Buildings, the Comte d'Angiviller, is not favorably inclined towards either Cochin or Chardin, whose pension is now cut down. Chardin exhibits three "head studies" in pastel at the Salon and paints the second "Self-Portrait" and the "Portrait of Madame Chardin" (both in the Louvre).

1775 Beaumarchais's "Barbier de Séville." Birth of Turner.

1776 Birth of Constable. American Declaration of Independence. Benjamin Franklin in Paris.

1776-1778 Rousseau's "Rêveries d'un promeneur solitaire."

1777 Chardin brings all his influence to bear in favor of Cochin, who under the new régime of Pierre and D'Angiviller has been relegated to an inferior position at the Academy—but in vain. Chardin exhibits three pastels and an oil at the Salon.

1778 Gainsborough's "Blue Boy." Death of Voltaire, Rousseau and Canaletto. Mesmerism all the rage in Paris.

1779 Chardin exhibits "several pastel studies of heads"—his last appearance at the Salon. The critics, though not enthusiastic, are full of indulgence for the "indefatigable old man." Following a visit of the Royal Family to the Salon, Madame Victoire buys one of Chardin's pastels and sends him a gold snuff-box.

September 25. Attends a meeting of the Academy for the last time.

November 16. The painter Doyen informs Desfriches that Chardin is very seriously ill. "He has received extreme unction and is in a state of collapse that makes us fear the worst. His mind is clear, but the swelling in his legs has spread to other parts of the body. There is no telling what turn his disorder will take."

December 6. Chardin dies in his apartment in the Louvre. Interred the next day at the church of Saint-Germain-l'Auxerrois. His death passed virtually unnoticed. Neoclassicism was at its height and his pictures had ceased to have any appeal.

1780 March 6. Chardin Sale at the Hôtel d'Aligre.

1780 Birth of Ingres.

JEAN SIMÉON CHARDIN

SELF-PORTRAIT WITH SPECTACLES. SIGNED AND DATED 1771.
PASTEL. LOUVRE, PARIS.

PORTRAIT OF CHARDIN

"MONSIEUR CHARDIN was small in stature, but strong and muscular." The painter was thus described by his friend Cochin, who spoke also of his "great store of good sense and excellent judgment." We can gather as much from the three self-portraits he painted late in life, in which there may still be glimpsed the *"homme d'esprit"* praised by Diderot. The face is open, shrewd, conscientious, and self-assured—and yet there is much about this self-taught, wonderfully gifted artist that remains a mystery.

Chardin was born on November 2, 1699, in the Rue de Seine, in the heart of Paris. His father, who was cabinetmaker to the King, apparently wished to have him follow in his footsteps or at any rate to become an artisan of some sort. He was, however, drawn towards painting, though it is not known how or when he first became aware of his vocation. After an apprenticeship in the studios of Pierre-Jacques Cazes and of Noël-Nicolas Coypel, he decided to strike out on his own. Throughout his life he was to regret his rather sketchy education, and on this account to hold a grudge against his father, who was deeply attached to his background and the traditions of his craft, considering membership of the Academy of St Luke to be the supreme achievement.

From the beginning, almost in spite of himself, Chardin went his own way, owing little to the official precepts of the Academy, and showing small inclination to be trained as one of those painters of historical scenes then considered to be the only real artists. Nor did he owe anything to Italy; he completed his training without any firsthand contact either with the art of classical antiquity or with that of the Italian masters of the Renaissance. It is true that Cazes taught him drawing and composition, but Cazes was limited by the hidebound academic outlook so typical of the more insipid followers of Lebrun, and painted from imagination rather than direct observation. Coypel, on the other hand, taught Chardin to *see*, encouraging the budding artist to use that gift of observation which the official teachings of the Academy might well have stifled.

About this early period of Chardin's life there remain only a few anecdotes, whose value is perhaps primarily symbolic. First of all, there is the story of the gun: Coypel (a friend of the family's since 1720) gave Chardin a gun to paint, placing it cunningly so as to catch the light. "It was then that he realized how difficult it is to achieve a faithful representation of color and the effects of light" (Cochin). He had to find his own solutions to the problem, to create his own inimitable manner.

Another, better authenticated anecdote shows the young artist taking the first step towards fame by painting a signboard for a "surgeon" friend of his father's. Of this, all that has survived is Jules de Goncourt's engraving after a sketch made at the time, but its originality and its almost "Venetian" touch at once brought his talent into prominence. It is certainly a curious coincidence that the two greatest French artists of the eighteenth century should each—though at an interval of some years—have painted a celebrated signboard!

In a third anecdote, we are told how the artist, not yet thirty and without the usual background, entered the Academy. And here the name of another notable painter crops up. Chardin assembled some of his latest pictures in a room at the Academy. Largillierre was struck by them, and thought they must be the work of a "Flemish master." Chardin confessed that he had painted them, and the great portraitist—who himself went in for still lifes, as may be seen from the recently published inventory of his works compiled at the time of his death (P. Grate, *La Revue du Louvre*, I, 1961, p. 30)—was so impressed that he urged the young man to present himself at the Academy forthwith. He was elected and received on the same day. *The Skate* and *The Sideboard* were the pictures that gained him acceptance. He was launched. All he had to do now was to consolidate his reputation and, once again, his faithful friend and biographer Cochin was at hand to record his progress.

A few years earlier Chardin had met a well-to-do girl. The betrothal contract had been signed, but the difference in their fortunes had been too marked and the young man insufficiently launched on his career to hope for an early marriage. But now he was a member of the Academy. In the meantime, as a result of the financial crisis in France at the end of Louis XIV's reign, the girl had lost her fortune. To the surprise of his contemporaries Chardin went through with the marriage.

The newlyweds had nothing to live on but the artist's canvases, and it was not a period favorable to the arts. Portraits were the only things that paid. Chardin was therefore obliged to do journeyman's work to make a living. It was at this point that, following Cazes, Coypel, and Largillierre, yet another artist friend was to lend a helping hand: Jean-Baptiste Van Loo, who had apparently known Chardin for several years. Commissioned to restore the paintings in the Galerie de François Ier at Fontainebleau, Van Loo employed Chardin as his assistant and paid him generously. But that was not all. He encouraged him by buying some of his pictures at prices beyond those he was asking for them.

Thus the various anecdotes of contemporary biographers present, step by step, the milestones in the artist's development.

Cazes: the rudiments of his craft, the art of drawing, copying. Coypel: the secrets of reality and its poetic portrayal, the importance of light and shadows. The signboard offers a link with Watteau. Largillierre: the most Chardinesque painter of still lifes before Chardin. Van Loo: the friend of the "lean years."

With Aved we come to the awakening of Chardin's interest in the portrayal of the human figure. The story goes as follows. Chardin was astonished to hear of the prices that Aved—an excellent portraitist who had lived for some time in Holland—could refuse for a portrait, prices that Chardin himself would have considered more than reasonable for his own still lifes. Aved observed rather caustically that it was much more difficult to paint a portrait than to paint a sausage. It was then that Chardin decided to apply himself to those little genre scenes that were to be no less masterly than his still lifes.

Each of these painters was more than a friend, he was a symbol. To Aved Chardin owed the introduction of the human figure into his pictures as well as his knowledge of the great Dutch masters, which is none the less profound for being indirect. In return, Chardin's portrait of his friend (now in the Louvre) was the most dazzling tribute that he could have paid not only to Aved, but to Rembrandt.

To speak of Chardin's life after 1730, when he may be said to have completed his apprenticeship to his art, is an easy, yet tricky task—easy because it is well documented, tricky because the essentials elude us. We know of the births of his son Pierre-Jean and of his daughter Marguerite-Agnès, of the death in 1735 of his ailing first wife whom he adored, of his daughter's death in childhood, of his remarriage in 1744 to a solid, robust widow Françoise-Marguerite Pouget, who was a great help to him in business matters. The misadventures of his son are also well known—how he too became a painter and obtained first prize at the Academy solely because of the esteem in which his father was held, how he tried in vain to make a success of his career, and how he committed suicide in Venice.

Then there was Chardin's loyalty to the Academy, where he exhibited his work regularly and climbed patiently from office to office (he could never become a professor, however, since he had entered as a painter specializing in animals and fruits, a minor genre whose practitioners were not permitted to teach).

There are also many stories of his influence in the world of art: how he had the privilege of hanging the works of his seniors, his rivals, his friends, and his juniors in the Salon Carré at the Louvre, of giving a favored position to those he liked, of hanging others in a dark corner where their weaknesses would escape an over-critical eye! And there was his mischievous wit that so delighted Diderot and other visitors to the Salon.

We also know about his friendship with various fellow academicians and the esteem in which they held him; his pleasure in talking "shop" with his colleagues, exchanging useful tips, discussing the tricks of the trade. We know about his deep friendship for Cochin, the all-powerful secretary of the Academy, to whom Chardin often gave his works to engrave, just as he had given them to Cochin's father—a friendship that never faltered even when Cochin fell into disfavor and was replaced by Jean-Baptiste Pierre.

We know the four different places he lived in: Rue de Seine, Rue Princesse at the corner of Rue du Four, Rue du Four itself, and finally the Louvre, where he died. There are inventories telling us the contents of his apartments. We know him too from his paintings in which the same objects are repeated over and over again. For example, the magnificent green stone jug that appears in *The Skate* (1728) was still intact several years later when he came to paint *The Copper Cistern*. Increasing affluence is reflected in his pictures by the appearance of finer glassware and more costly household objects.

We know the story of the last difficult years—his declining health, his failing eyesight that obliged him to try out a new technique, that of the pastel. Like his friend Cochin he was to fall on evil days. His works ceased to fetch such high prices, and he was obliged to relinquish his duties at the Academy and sell his house. But he never gave up. We know his tenacity in his quarrels with the new Director General of Buildings, and his tenacity in teaching himself to work in pastels. And we know that his sense of humor remained with him to the end. "That picture-hanger Chardin (an allusion to his duties at the Salon) is a first-class wag. He is never so delighted as when he is up to some prank" (Diderot). And he was also a stickler for neatness, taking the same pride in his appearance on his deathbed as he had taken throughout his life: "During his last illness he always had himself shaved as usual," and the author of the *Mémoires secrets* ends his eulogy with the following striking observation: "He used to say that the hand and the palette are needed in order to paint, but that a painting is not made with the hand and the palette."

All this is known, and yet the essential Chardin cannot be pinned down. Where did he learn his wonderful craftsmanship, and how did he acquire his amazing skill at composition and his feeling for the simple everyday object? Why did he produce no landscapes and leave behind no drawings that can be unreservedly accepted? There is much that is obscure in the career of this simple, homely artist, and it may be that his secrets are hidden in his very simplicity. An examination of his works and his artistic achievement will perhaps shed light on the mystery.

HIS TECHNIQUE AND HIS MASTERS

CHARDIN'S career opened with two bombshells: *The Skate* and *The Sideboard*. There was also, of course, the signboard showing "a surgeon-barber in his shop bandaging a man wounded in a duel," but both the original and the sketch have now disappeared, the first temporarily perhaps, the second irrevocably destroyed by fire. This youthful work certainly appears to have been exceptional. Nothing could be more unexpected than the street scene, taken straight from life, whose lively, humorous treatment is so admirably rendered in Jules de Goncourt's etching, but it seems to have been unique in Chardin's work.

The Skate and *The Sideboard* were both painted before 1728. What was there so new in these two masterly paintings, which demonstrate—perhaps with a certain over-emphasis, a certain provocative exaggeration—a number of the artist's special qualities? To answer this question we need to know something about the still life before Chardin.

The French still life painters of the seventeenth century, particularly those of the period of Louis XIII (1610-1643), are today enjoying renewed popularity. They represent in fact the only aspect of French art in the seventeenth century—apart from Georges de La Tour, and certainly far more than Poussin or the Parisian masters of the Regency period—which today appeals to the general public. But Chardin's work has nothing in common with the minute detail, frigid precision and complicated symbolism of their still lifes, in which each object stands apart, distinct from the ones next to it—nothing except perhaps for a like simplicity of composition, a like discretion and restraint vis-à-vis the objects portrayed.

His own special contribution was to be a subtle interplay of light and shade, a softening of the outlines, a "breaking up" of tones, and a concern for masses, for overall effect. Here he may owe a partial debt to certain of his seniors: Alexandre-François Desportes (1666-1743), two copies of whose work were surprisingly enough owned by Chardin, and Jean-Baptiste Oudry (1686-1755). But the productions of these two academic painters, though sumptuous and brilliant, and frequently enlivened by dogs, birds, and anecdotal elements, were primarily decorative still lifes, whereas Chardin was to be the great master of the *still* life in the most literal sense of the term.

One painter already referred to, who is rarely mentioned in connection with Chardin's development, nevertheless seems to have had a decisive influence on his work: Nicolas de Largillierre (1656-1746). This influence was exercised not so much through his formal portraits of the wealthy middle classes—although the portrayal of shimmering silks and rich brocades is not so far removed from that of wet fruit gleaming in a bowl of glass— as through the "Flemish" still lifes of his youth, of which an example may be seen in the museum at Amiens (the epithet "Flemish" was often applied to Chardin himself, and is certainly justified in connection with Largillierre when we remember that he was brought up in Antwerp and trained there). Although there is nothing to indicate that Chardin served an apprenticeship in Largillierre's studio, he was to assimilate the lesson of the master more thoroughly than his actual pupils (such as Oudry), and to complete it with the addition of his own genius. Largillierre's were the first French still lifes to come alive, and while his handling may seem dull and poverty-stricken when set

LADY SEALING A LETTER. SIGNED AND DATED 1733.
STAATLICHE SCHLÖSSER UND GÄRTEN, BERLIN.

LADY DRINKING TEA. SIGNED AND DATED 1738.
HUNTERIAN COLLECTION, UNIVERSITY OF GLASGOW.

beside Chardin's lavish and delectable impasto, he nevertheless imparted to his subjects something of the same calm, restful life.

It must be remembered that Largillierre was a theorist as well as a painter, and Oudry paid tribute to him as such in two lectures at the Academy. That "local color" which he defined as being natural to each object, and as something distinct from "chiaroscuro" which is "the art of distributing light and shade," is to be found in Chardin, who employed the same terms when acting as Diderot's guide at the Salons.

While these French influences were fundamental to Chardin's development, they are not the only keys to an understanding of his style. The artist—and in this he was typical of his period—had a lively curiosity. Early eighteenth-century Paris was a rich and populous city, where numerous collectors freely opened the doors of their "cabinets" (as private collections were called) to foreign artists and their work. Thus Chardin certainly had every opportunity to make up for anything he might have learnt by studying at the Academy and visiting Italy.

Of the curiosity just mentioned there is ample evidence in Chardin's friendships with the more cultured of his colleagues, his keen interest in everything relating to the technical side of his craft, his active participation in the affairs of the Academy, and the pictures which he is known to have owned, modest works no doubt, but indicative of his friendships and his taste: a sketch by Watteau, pictures by La Hyre and Jouvenet, copies of Lebrun and Desportes, sculptures by Pigalle, and drawings by Cochin. It is not surprising therefore that his work should testify to a wealth of outside influences, some of them obvious, others less so.

The eighteenth century saw Chardin as an imitator of the Flemish painters. The nineteenth century, while mentioning the Le Nain brothers in the same breath, compared him to the little masters of seventeenth-century Dutch painting. This contradiction is, however, more apparent than real. To Largillierre, who himself drew upon the Flemish tradition, Chardin was certainly a painter in that tradition. This opinion was shared by that enlightened art-lover and collector La Live de Jully, who commissioned him to paint "a 'Grace before Meat' as a companion piece to a Teniers." Chardin's monkey pictures, like those of Watteau, are in fact pastiches in the French manner of similar subjects by Teniers, and moreover the least attractive part of his work. In 1748, a connoisseur, Abbé Gougenot, dubbed him "the French Teniers," adding, however, that he found him "more exact in drawing, more refined and delicate in expression."

While such comparisons may seem today unwarranted, it is none the less certain that Chardin inclined towards the Flemish school in his predilection for paintings of laden sideboards, a genre greatly appreciated in France through the works of Jan Fyt, Frans Snyders, and their many French imitators who were so much in vogue in the time of Louis XIV. *The Skate* and *The Sideboard* are the most representative works of the artist in this sumptuous genre, whose secrets he certainly understood, although its opulence ran counter to his temperament. Our admiration of the two works which gained the young man admittance to the Academy is tempered with a certain reluctance, for he seems to have used them primarily as showpieces for his precocious technical skill and to have put too little of himself into them. An artist of Chardin's calibre soon outgrows this kind of exhibitionism.

In his attempts to imitate the little masters of seventeenth-century Holland, so popular among the collectors of the period, he did not seem any the less "Flemish" to his contemporaries, who used the term to cover the Low Countries as well as Flanders. His knowledge of the minor Dutch masters was undoubtedly due to his good friend Aved, who was known as "the Batavian" because he had lived in Holland, and who was also a discriminating collector of Dutch paintings. The *Lady sealing a Letter*, painted some five years after the two great still lifes, at first sight appears to be a large-scale version of a work by Gerard Dou. Yet we are far removed here from the polished, ironic, rather literary canvases of the Dutch painter. In the very personal melancholy of this exceptionally large composition, in the suspended gesture, the silence that goes beyond mere anecdote, Chardin succeeded at the very first attempt in revitalizing a theme that had seemed to be played out.

The general public was to know this work only through the engraving made by Fessard in 1738. This was printed with some heavy-handed explanatory lines that would seem to bring it down to the level of a picture that "tells a story":

> "Hâte-toi donc, Frontin, vois ta jeune maîtresse
> Sa tendre impatience éclate dans ses yeux;
> Il lui tarde déjà que l'objet de ses vœux
> Ait reçu ce billet, gage de sa tendresse.
> Ah! Frontin, pour agir avec cette lenteur
> Jamais le Dieu d'Amour n'a donc touché ton cœur?"

("Make haste, Frontin. Behold your young mistress whose tender impatience sparkles in her eyes; she cannot wait for the object of her desires to receive this note, a pledge of her affection. Ah, Frontin, if you act so slowly the God of Love has surely never touched your heart.")

Certainly the eighteenth-century approach to this fine composition—in which Chardin expresses himself so much more quietly and subtly than in the superabundant sparkle and liveliness of the two great "sideboard pieces"—was very different from ours.

Chardin, however, owed an even greater debt to Holland (again, no doubt, thanks to Aved): the influence of Rembrandt. Flickering, broken, tortured and tortuous, Chardin's brushwork is unique in eighteenth-century French art, having none of the fluent ease and smoothness that is to be found, for example, in Boucher. Thick, oily, endlessly worked over, heavy or light to excess, his paints seem at times to have been smeared over the surface of the canvas. With the sumptuous texture—and at times the calculation—of rich abstract colors, his brushwork harks back to Claude Vignon at the beginning of the seventeenth century and above all to Rembrandt. It is true that Rembrandt's effects are gloomy and dramatic, while Chardin's are just the opposite, but surely the style is the same after the lapse of a century, though employed to different ends.

In 1734 Chardin painted a portrait of Aved as "A Chemist in his Laboratory," and there is something extremely touching

LADY DRINKING TEA, DETAIL. SIGNED AND DATED 1738.
HUNTERIAN COLLECTION, UNIVERSITY OF GLASGOW.

in this appropriate tribute to the man who had introduced him to Rembrandt's work. Twenty years later, when this portrait —made famous in the meantime by Bernard Lépicié's engraving (1742)—was exhibited at the Salon of 1753 under the title "Philosopher Reading," Huquier the Younger made the following comment: "For the general effect it could be put on a level with Rembrandt, but the accuracy and fineness of the drawing raise it to an even higher level."

Whether or not Chardin had the opportunity to perfect his knowledge through contact with those Italian masters who then were celebrated throughout Europe is a point on which the biographers are silent. Two contemporary writers, however, touched on the matter. In reviewing the Salon of 1761 the rather uninspired critic of the *Mercure de France* wrote with reference to Chardin: "For all their patience the Dutch did not copy nature more exactly, and for all their genius the Italians did not render it with a more vigorous brush"; while the writer of a lengthy obituary notice on the painter stated that "he kept a watchful eye on the masterpieces of modern Italy." Moreover, the frequent visits of Venetian painters to England obliged them to pass through Paris. Before closing this chapter on influences, may we diffidently put forward the names of Giuseppe Maria Crespi and of Giovanni Battista Piazzetta, the latter being Chardin's senior by sixteen years? Perhaps one day a definite link will be established between these names and Chardin's, or perhaps it is all a matter of coincidence like that miraculous link across the years between Chardin and his kindred spirit, Vermeer of Delft.

Coincidence or not, if ever an eighteenth-century artist painted in a manner closely resembling Chardin's, that painter was Piazzetta.

THE ART OF CHARDIN

SLICED MELON. SIGNED, UNDATED, LOUVRE, PARIS.

CHARDIN AND THE IMAGINATION

"H IS progress was so rapid that no interval appears to have elapsed between his first work and his last." The lack of development in Chardin's work is thus described by one of his contemporaries; technical development, that is, for his subject matter certainly varied in the course of his career. His early still lifes followed one another in rapid succession—Georges Wildenstein has reckoned that a quarter of his total output was produced before 1732. Then, from 1733 onwards, figures began to appear in his paintings, a development approved of by many of his contemporaries, although one of them, the collector and connoisseur Pierre-Jean Mariette, had some rather biting comments to make in this connection: "Chardin was afraid, and perhaps rightly so, that if he went on painting only inanimate, not very interesting objects, the public would soon tire of his work, whereas if he turned his hand to live animals, he would not be able to do so well as Desportes and Oudry, two strong rivals who had been first in the field and whose reputations were established." In this new genre, Chardin painted some of his most popular works, while continuing with his still lifes and producing his first portraits.

When Diderot wrote of him, Chardin was at the height of his powers and the peak of his fame. He was commissioned to paint overdoor panels for the royal châteaux of Choisy and Bellevue. However, from 1733 onwards, his output slackened. His contemporaries often took him to task for his laziness. Certainly

THE BRIOCHE, ALSO CALLED A DESSERT. SIGNED AND DATED 1763.
LOUVRE, PARIS.

it took time to paint as he did, but this is hardly an adequate explanation. Here we may cite Lecomte and Coypel, writing in 1751: "The public is vexed never to see more than one work from his skillful brush. I have heard that he is working on a new one and I have been greatly intrigued by its unusual theme.

It shows him in front of a canvas on an easel. His brushes are being handed to him by a little Genius representing Nature. As he takes them Fortune snatches some of them away and, contemplating the indolent smile of Sloth, he lets the rest fall from his hands."

A few pastels complete this straightforward simple career in which imagination and variety of subject matter seem to have played but little part: Chardin was not an artist who moved from phase to phase.

PEACH, PLUMS, BISCUITS, BOTTLE AND EARTHENWARE JAR ON A TABLE.
MUSÉE DES BEAUX-ARTS, ANGERS.

His very personal style, which owes so much to the heavy, richly textured brushwork, may explain why there are so few drawings that can be attributed to him with any certainty. We know that, like everyone else at the time, he had been taught to draw. Diderot quotes him as follows: "At the age of seven or eight, we have pencil-holders thrust into our hands. We start copying eyes, mouths, noses, ears, then feet and hands. After spending interminable hours huddled over our sketchbooks, we are set in front of a Hercules or a Torso, and you cannot conceive how many tears that Satyr, that Gladiator, that Medici Venus, and that Antinous have caused to flow."

We know from the inventory compiled after his death that he left several albums containing hundreds of drawings, but it is not known whether these were his own—as we suspect them to have been—or works by his friends. While a few unfinished pictures showing Chardin's method of composing by large masses have survived, we know of no preliminary study for a painting that can be unreservedly attributed to him. This is hardly surprising—preliminary studies for still lifes are extremely rare, although Oudry left some excellent ones. With Chardin's very special method of working, moreover, such studies were more or less out of the question. Mariette, who was not over-fond of Chardin and who was too great a lover of drawings to appreciate an artist who did not produce any, was clear on this point: "Not being sufficiently versed in drawing to make preliminary studies on paper, Monsieur Chardin is obliged to keep his subject before his eyes from the first outline to the last stroke of the brush."

Chardin was "obliged to keep his subject before his eyes"; this phrase holds one of the keys to his art. Chardin worked from the model, directly "from life." In the opinion of Mariette, who in the last analysis cared only for history painting, this was, if not a defect, at least a limitation, as is made clear by his scornful use of the word "obliged." To his way of thinking, only imaginative painting—that is, the pictorial transcription of an idea by means of an original composition based on drawings, sketches, and models, but conceived in the mind of the artist—had any true nobility. Artists like Desportes and Oudry made drawings of plants and animals from life, but when they came to paint

BASKET OF PEACHES.
CHESTER DALE COLLECTION, NATIONAL GALLERY OF ART, WASHINGTON.

THE SILVER GOBLET. SIGNED. LOUVRE, PARIS.

they relied on their imagination, prompted at most by their preliminary drawings. In the opinion of Mariette and other contemporaries, Chardin was a mere "copyist." His remarkable and inimitable technique and his admirable sense of composition went only halfway towards redeeming this capital "defect."

Of Chardin's incapacity to paint from the imagination—an incapacity which he turned to wonderful account—we have ample evidence in some of the copies signed by his own hand. Several such copies of his more successful works were commissioned by wealthy art-lovers, but, being based on memory rather than life, they were painted without affection, and show it.

This limitation was cruelly insisted upon by a number of eighteenth-century critics, who spoke of Chardin's perfection "in his genre," by which they referred as much to his habit of working from life as to the type of picture he painted. Their idea of great art was to take a subject such as the martyrdom of St Stephen and make something original out of it. Chardin no doubt suffered grievously from this attitude, yet his approach has been amply justified in the eyes of posterity. It was not by chance that interest in Chardin revived just when the Impressionists were beginning to rediscover nature by planting their easels firmly in front of it. While his composition anticipated Cézanne and his brushwork stimulated Van Gogh, it was his approach to the object by direct observation that won him the plaudits of the Impressionists.

Chardin painted from life. His models were the household articles that surrounded him, and he used them over and over again. One author has gone so far as to assert that, from the inventories that survive and, above all, from the pictures, it would be easy to reconstruct the Chardin household down to its smallest details. We can date to the year the disappearance of the green jug, possibly as a result of Madame Chardin's clumsiness. We can date the appearance of the silver goblet bought to mark some special occasion. How small Chardin's world appears to be, and how limited his imagination. His gift lay, however, in quite another direction. It was, in the highest degree, that of conferring distinction upon the homely object and of finding in it a whole universe, the boundless universe of the poet.

THE DRAFTSMAN. SIGNED AND DATED 1737. STAATLICHE MUSEEN, BERLIN.

COMPOSITION AND EMOTIONAL EXPRESSION

Leaving aside the portraits in oils and the pastels, Chardin's pictures can be classified in three groups: figure paintings, still lifes of objects, and still lifes of game. The illustrations in this book offer a regrouping of these themes, with which Chardin dealt more or less concurrently throughout his career.

The first category includes the series of half-length figures, undoubtedly the finest being the *Lady sealing a Letter* (Berlin), the *Lady drinking Tea* (Glasgow), and the Berlin version of *The Draftsman*. It also includes a second group of subtly handled interiors: *The Laundress* and *The Draftsman* (Stockholm), *The Scullery Maid* and *The Cellar Boy* (Glasgow), *Saying Grace* and especially the *Return from Market*, in which the same impression of silence, the same suspended gestures can be found.

Take, for example, the Berlin version of *The Draftsman*, which is particularly revealing in this respect. Wearing a cocked hat and a wig, the young artist is bending attentively over a drawing, apparently a caricature, which he has just finished. He holds a freshly pared stick of chalk and a knife. His portfolio of drawings is lying on the table, placed at a slight angle to the edge, in order to relieve its geometrical severity. To this first break in the pattern of the composition, Chardin has cunningly added a second—the knotted ribbon on the portfolio. The face with its relaxed, reflective calm, is of a type that Chardin used again and again, yet with nothing wearisome in the repetition.

SAYING GRACE. UNDATED. LOUVRE, PARIS.

THE MORNING TOILET. UNDATED. NATIONALMUSEUM, STOCKHOLM.

GIRL WITH A SHUTTLECOCK. SIGNED. UFFIZI, FLORENCE.

It is found again in such domestic scenes as *Saying Grace* at the Louvre (which owns two versions of this work), and *The Morning Toilet* and *The Laundress* (Stockholm)—pictures of such exquisite taste that there is something almost irksome in their

CHILD WITH A TOP (PORTRAIT OF AUGUSTE-GABRIEL GODEFROY).
SIGNED, DATE ILLEGIBLE. LOUVRE, PARIS.

perfection—and again in the admirable replica of the *Girl with a Shuttlecock*, acquired by the Uffizi in 1951, and in the *Child with a Top* at the Louvre. These pictures have one special element in common: a profound feeling for childhood and its pastimes that is not shared by many other artists. In this connection Charles Sterling has written: "Chardin is one of the great painters of children," adding: "Most of his domestic scenes were made for them and are seen from their point of view. The adults appear to be living in a different world." His pictures of childhood—grave, calm, and absorbed—are pictures of a world that Jean-Jacques Rousseau was one of the first to explore.

In all these paintings we find the same assured composition, the same thick and clotted brushwork that can convey the weave of a fabric as well as the rough surface of a whitewashed wall. Take, for example, the small Stockholm version of *The Drafts-man*, brother to the Berlin one. The young artist has a similar folder of drawings and is wearing the same cocked hat. He is sitting on the floor copying a Daumier-like nude fastened to the wall by two nails. To reinforce the rather fluid composition of this tiny picture, Chardin has placed a skillful geometrical arrangement in the upper right-hand corner. It reminds us of another portrayal of a draftsman in his studio, this time a rich and crowded one, with paintings covering the walls: the picture in the Vienna Academy by Pierre Subleyras (1699-1749), a French artist enamored of Rome, of the stately classical art of the seventeenth century, and of rich paintwork.

The same in-gathered silence and suspended gestures are to be found in *The Cellar Boy* and *The Scullery Maid* (Glasgow), and in that astonishing achievement the *Return from Market* (the finest version of which is undoubtedly the one in the Louvre). How subtly the pyramidal central figure is balanced by the recession of planes and the interplay of the half-opened doors that plunge one room in shadow and flood the other with light.

THE DRAFTSMAN. SIGNED. WOOD.
NATIONALMUSEUM, STOCKHOLM.

THE CELLAR BOY. SIGNED AND DATED 1738.
HUNTERIAN COLLECTION, UNIVERSITY OF GLASGOW.

THE SCULLERY MAID. SIGNED AND DATED 1738.
HUNTERIAN COLLECTION, UNIVERSITY OF GLASGOW.

THE CELLAR BOY, DETAIL. SIGNED AND DATED 1738.
HUNTERIAN COLLECTION, UNIVERSITY OF GLASGOW.

THE SCULLERY MAID, DETAIL. SIGNED AND DATED 1738.
HUNTERIAN COLLECTION, UNIVERSITY OF GLASGOW.

RETURN FROM MARKET, DETAIL. SIGNED AND DATED 1739. LOUVRE, PARIS.

And yet when Lépicié came to make an engraving of the *Return from Market* in 1742 he could find nothing better to put beneath it than these lines:

"A votre air, j'estime et je pense,
Ma chère enfant, sans calculer,
Que vous prenez sur la dépense
Ce qu'il faut pour vous habiller."

RETURN FROM MARKET, DETAIL. SIGNED AND DATED 1739. LOUVRE, PARIS.

THE LAUNDRESS. SIGNED, UNDATED. NATIONALMUSEUM, STOCKHOLM.

Which may be roughly rendered as follows:

> By your appearance, I should say,
> Dear child, that you contrive to pay
> For those becoming clothes you wear
> With money meant for household fare.

RETURN FROM MARKET. SIGNED AND DATED 1739. LOUVRE, PARIS.

We know to what extent prints helped to popularize Chardin's work, and his friendship with the two Cochins (both of them engravers) was in a sense a business partnership. Yet we cannot but be astonished to learn what the eighteenth century actually saw in Chardin, as revealed in these facetious lines which make a feeble joke out of what—for us—is an admirable piece of painting. In the nineteenth century, critical opinion led by the Goncourt brothers, saw the same work as a portrait of a Parisian *bourgeoise*, proud, hard-working and quick-witted, one of those strong-minded, independent women whose sons were to bring about the Revolution. As for the twentieth century, we have only to turn to André Malraux, in the *Voices of Silence*, for a contemporary summing up of the scope and significance of this work: "The housewife in the *Return from Market* is a first-class Braque, dressed up just enough to deceive the onlooker." But is this view any more final? Surely the greatness of the picture lies in the fact that it has had something to say to each succeeding generation in terms of that generation's own concerns.

Turning to the still lifes, we find the same qualities. The silent presence of the objects depicted is disturbed only rarely by the intrusion of a live animal (the cat in *The Skate* and the dog in *The Sideboard* were in fact put in simply out of deference to his great Flemish and French predecessors in the domain of still life painting and hardly add to the reputation of the artist). That silent presence is akin to the mysterious stillness of his human figures, whether children or adults. How, then, did Chardin approach the subject matter of his still lifes? Consider, for example, *The Copper Cistern*, whose exact date is unknown, but which seems to have been painted no later than 1733. It shows a cistern similar to the one that stands on a tripod in the background of the *Return from Market*, but this time viewed from the front. A bucket filled with water stands under the

THE COPPER CISTERN. SIGNED, UNDATED. WOOD. LOUVRE, PARIS.

tap; to the right there is a green stone jug with its lid placed beside it on the ground; to the left, a long-handled saucepan is leaning against a magnificent grey wall, from which the massive bulk of the cistern stands out. The range of colors is as restricted as possible: a few copper tones from the brightest of golds to the deepest glint of reddish brown, a dark green, a symphony of greys. On closer inspection, it can be seen that

THE JAR OF OLIVES. SIGNED AND DATED 1760. LOUVRE, PARIS.

THE MAKINGS OF A LUNCH, OR THE REMAINS OF A LUNCH.
SIGNED AND DATED (DATE ALMOST ILLEGIBLE). LOUVRE, PARIS.

every splash of bright color (the saucepan) is balanced by a corresponding dark mass (the green jug).

The basic composition—in particular, the line-up of the saucepan, bucket and jug—might seem a little crude. However, the jug lid, placed on the ground a little in front of the other

THE JAR OF OLIVES, DETAIL. SIGNED AND DATED 1760. LOUVRE, PARIS.

objects, provided an excellent counterpoint. The artist did not stop at that, but softened all the masses by a few details that infuse rhythm into the composition (the handles of the cistern, its tap, the loop for hanging up the saucepan), thus removing a cubist element too outrageous for the graceful taste of the period. Then he balanced his colors: "He went over all the shadows again," wrote Cochin, "whatever color they were." "When the picture is done," Chardin himself said, "it must be gone over once again with these colors (those already employed) in order to harmonize it." Harmony is a word that can be applied to every picture by Chardin, and indeed a surprisingly large number of musical terms can be aptly used to describe his work. But did this "precursor of Cubism" act consciously? Or did his genius reside in his repertoire of technical tricks?

Describing the *Jar of Olives* exhibited at the Salon of 1763, Diderot made the following perceptive comments:

"The artist has placed an old china bowl on the table, together with two biscuits, a jar containing olives, a basket of fruit, two half-filled wine glasses, a Seville orange, and a meat pie.

"To look at pictures by other artists, it seems that I need to borrow a different pair of eyes. To look at those of Chardin, I have only to keep the eyes Nature gave me and make good use of them.

"For the china bowl is of real china, the olives are actually separated from the eye by the water in which they are steeped, one has only to pick up the biscuits and eat them, to cut open the orange and squeeze it, to drink the glass of wine, peel the fruit, take up a knife and slice the pie.

"Nobody has a greater understanding of the harmony of color and reflections. Ah, Chardin, what you grind on your palette is not this color or that, red, black, or white, but the very substance of things. You dip your brush in air and light and spread them on your canvas."

All is said, nothing explained. Such mastery does not come from the application of some set theory of painting; the work creates the principle, but is not based on it.

The same unaffected skill is found in the small canvas in the Louvre called *The Kitchen Table*. The table edge might have seemed too unrelievedly straight, so the artist placed a leek on

THE COPPER CAULDRON. SIGNED. WOOD. MUSÉE COGNACQ-JAY, PARIS.

it. The side of the table is in shadow. The delicate white stem of the leek stands out against it, while the green part is laid on the bright surface of the table, which sheds a glow on all the objects placed upon it. There would be something rather disconcerting about such simple technical devices as these, if their very simplicity, not to say naivety, did not carry the artist to sublime heights and enable him to show up the over-studied compositions of his brother-artists. Set side by side with those of Chardin, the paintings of his contemporaries are all too often revealed as insipid decorative works, painful in their laboriousness.

The same device is used in *The Copper Cauldron* in the Cognacq-Jay Museum. This is a companion piece to *The Kitchen Table* in the Louvre (both works, or at least two pictures exactly the same, belonged to Chardin's engraver and friend, Wille, who bought them for thirty-six francs in 1760, when the artist was at the peak of his fame); here a knife serves the same purpose as the leek in the companion painting.

The secret of Chardin's art has been admirably expressed by a very different painter, namely Delacroix, who did not particularly care for the art of the eighteenth century and was not consciously referring to Chardin when he wrote in his *Journal*: "When we look at the objects around us, we observe a sort of *liaison* between them, produced by the atmosphere that envelops them and by all kinds of reflections which somehow make each of them partake of a general harmony... Yet how few of the great masters have been concerned with this."

The last statement is perfectly true, and it is astonishing to find these two painters, who could not have been more different, agreeing on the crucial question of what constitutes harmony in a work of art. How did Chardin achieve his consummate harmony? A clue is provided by A. de Ridder, writing in 1932: "With Chardin, the canvas, generally of medium grain and covered with a heavy priming coat, in every way facilitated that superimposition of layers of paint that characterizes his manner." The canvas was first primed with size, then a thin coat of oil color (usually a mixture of white lead and reddish brown) was applied, thus giving the artist a dark ground and a solid foundation on which he could start work straight away.

THE MAKINGS OF A LUNCH, OR THE REMAINS OF A LUNCH, DETAIL.
SIGNED AND DATED (DATE ALMOST ILLEGIBLE). LOUVRE, PARIS.

FLOWER PIECE. UNDATED.
NATIONAL GALLERY OF SCOTLAND, EDINBURGH.

First of all he painted in the dark parts of his picture, then he put the half-tones over them, added a lighter tone here and there, and finally went over the bright as well as the dark parts again to achieve, after patient and painstaking labor, those flawless harmonies that he alone was able to create.

BASKET OF GRAPES WITH APPLES, TWO BISCUITS AND A PEAR. SIGNED AND DATED 1764. MUSÉE DES BEAUX-ARTS, ANGERS.

TWO WILD RABBITS WITH GAME-BAG AND POWDER-FLASK,
ALSO CALLED THE RETURN FROM THE HUNT. MUSÉE DE PICARDIE, AMIENS.

"Chardin's great secret lay precisely in his subtle range of
related tones. To all appearances scarcely varied, they are actually
seen to be, on closer inspection, a blend of many delicate shades,
though in the end they fuse into an over-all harmony. The
painter achieves this unity by his skillful handling of reflections,

TWO RABBITS AND A PHEASANT. SIGNED, UNDATED.
SAMUEL H. KRESS COLLECTION, NATIONAL GALLERY OF ART, WASHINGTON.

each color acting to some extent as a mirror to another, shading
off imperceptibly, over-vivid contrasts being avoided or imme-
diately attenuated."

Yet this impassive, calculated art can be surprisingly moving,
and nowhere more so than in the presence of death, which

HARE WITH A COPPER CAULDRON, A QUINCE AND TWO CHESTNUTS.
INITIALED. NATIONALMUSEUM, STOCKHOLM.

Chardin depicted with such restraint. The astonishing little *Wild Rabbits*, freshly killed, in the museum of Amiens (Chardin—who, like Soutine, worked slowly—must just have had time to finish them before they started to decay), the *Two Rabbits and Pheasant* in Washington, the large *Hare* in Stockholm, hanging by the paws, its blood staining the ground and interacting, in a strange blend of cruelty and refinement, with the acid yellow of the quince beside it: these count among the best still lifes ever painted. In them the French term *nature morte* finds an expression as exact as it is tragic.

For Chardin was no cold-blooded technician. His was a deeply emotional nature, kept deliberately under control in his art, though the spray of orange blossom in *The Brioche* and the *Flower Piece* reminiscent of Manet, now in the Edinburgh museum, show this control being strained to the utmost.

The two pastel self-portraits, whose rough strength has been so perfectly described by Marcel Proust, confirm this impression. The careful draftsman of impassive faces, the skilled craftsman juggling with forms and colors, lights and shadows, placing a leek or a knife with artful casualness on a table edge that would otherwise be too uncompromisingly straight, concealed a deeply sensitive and tender-hearted man, a member of that "aristocracy of the people" spoken of by Germain Bazin—and also of that aristocracy of painters, the Vermeers, the Corots, whose unpretentious, understated works may not attract the plaudits of the crowd, but earn the esteem of the discriminating few. And thanks to these works, a simple cooking utensil standing in the sun, an orange, or a half-empty wine glass can take on their original beauty for us once more.

HARE WITH A COPPER CAULDRON, A QUINCE AND TWO CHESTNUTS, DETAIL.
INITIALED. NATIONALMUSEUM, STOCKHOLM.

CHARDIN'S BRUSHWORK
SOME FRIENDS AND ADMIRERS

CHARDIN'S handling of paint is undoubtedly the aspect of his work that, from his own day to ours, has most impressed his admirers. Even more than his choice of subject matter, his balanced composition and his tranquil poetry, it is this that has given his work a place apart. As long ago as 1763 Diderot wrote: "There is no way of explaining this magic—thick layers of color are applied one upon another, and their effect seeps through from the first layer to the last... Go closer, and the picture blurs, flattens out, and disappears. Step back, and it is created anew, takes shape again."

Let us go closer then and, with the aid of enlarged details from characteristic still lifes, try to analyse the secret of that technique whereby the frail integument of the everyday object was recreated in the thickest of paint. "If you look closely, you will see red in the glass of water, red in the blue apron, blue in the white cloth. It is from these links, these continual echoes that all his paintings derive the harmony that strikes us from a distance—not the thin harmony of blending tones, but the full harmony of consonances that only the hand of a master can achieve" (Goncourt).

Chardin's proverbial slowness is explained by this very individual technique, by the way in which he handled his impasto, kneading it, reworking it, linking the color effects until perfection was achieved. In view of this, it seems hardly probable that all of the 1200 paintings attributed to him are by his own hand. An average of two pictures a month seems rather a high one for Chardin, particularly when we remember that, according to a contemporary who knew him well, he never had more than one in progress at a given time and that he was "not overfond of hard work" (Cochin).

In his own day, his love of fine rich pigments was celebrated and he was accordingly consulted by the Academy on such problems as a new formula for carmine (1765) or the utility of two natural earth colors—"yellow ochre" and "red-brown ochre"—that had been found "on the estates of the Baron de la Lézardière" (1771). It is his handling of paint, his brushwork, combined with his great distinction of mind, rather than the originality of his subject matter, that gives Chardin the right to be considered, after Watteau, as "the other great independent of the century" (Charles Sterling). Watteau deliberately turned his back on the followers of Lebrun (though in the latter's admirable *Grace before Meat* at the Louvre the plate of apples on the edge of the table is worthy of Chardin himself) and on the traditions established by the great master of the decorations at Versailles. The kind of art personified by Chardin has little in common with that officially favored, such as the "sugary" decorative works of Boucher's imitators. David was the third great artistic personality of the eighteenth century, which was much more varied than is customarily thought. Watteau, Chardin, and David—a period that had room for three such non-conformist painters must be considered astonishingly rich. Set beside those artists who are rightly or wrongly considered as symbols of the age—Boucher, Hubert Robert, Fragonard, and Greuze—Chardin seems to be an isolated figure. In this, he may be likened to Gabriel de Saint-Aubin, that fastidious master, who had all the curiosity and elegance of his period, together with an uneasy morbid streak that paved the way for the daring innovations of the nineteenth century.

Certainly Chardin had his imitators. And, leaving aside the delicate and as yet scarcely investigated matter of the replicas and second versions that filled his studio, we can name a number of them: they ranged from Etienne Aubry to Jeaurat (or rather, the Jeaurats—Etienne, of course, and Nicolas-Henri), from Henri Horace Roland de la Porte, undoubtedly the most gifted of all, to the estimable Bachelier, from Bounieu to Anne Vallayer-Coster, from Lépicié to Françoise Duparc. But none of these painters, some of whom have not more than ten known works to their credit, can hold a candle to the master. Sometimes they lapse into the anecdotal, the narrative, or the picturesque, all of which Chardin—fortunately for his reputation today—so skillfully avoided. In their still lifes, they tended to carry on the tradition of Desportes and Oudry (whose studio was taken over after his death by his son Jacques), and their work was little more than decorative—attractive and expert, it is true, but lacking the fine classical severity of the master. Melendez, working in the Spanish tradition, was probably the only eighteenth-century artist to approach Chardin's harmonious genius, though he was not actually influenced by him.

To think of Chardin as a solitary figure in that prolific age might make us imagine that he was personally isolated, too. But this was not at all so. He is known to have had a wide circle of friends, and we often find his signature together with Madame Chardin's added to letters from Cochin to, say, Desfriches. His rooms at the Louvre, between those of Hubert Robert and Joseph Vernet, who were also friends of his, though rather younger, set him at the center of the artistic life of his day. The names most frequently mentioned in connection with Chardin include: the engraver Wille, Desfriches (a draftsman from Orleans), Jean-Baptiste Van Loo, Jean-Baptiste Descamps the painter, the brilliant Cochin, Joseph Vernet, Hubert Robert, the pastellist Maurice Quentin de La Tour,

TWO RABBITS AND A PHEASANT, DETAIL. SIGNED, UNDATED.
SAMUEL H. KRESS COLLECTION, NATIONAL GALLERY OF ART, WASHINGTON.

Michel-Jean Sedaine (author of *Le Philosophe sans le savoir* and *Rose et Colas*, so popular at the time), the sculptor Jean-Baptiste Pigalle, the engraver Le Bas—men of varying ages, an odd, mixed set, bound by some mysterious link, beyond their professional interests, whose exact nature eludes us.

THE COPPER CAULDRON, DETAIL. WOOD. MUSÉE COGNACQ-JAY, PARIS.

Were Chardin's friends aware of the exceptional place he occupied in the art of his period? This is rather a delicate question. The critics were always, or nearly always, full of praise for his work. He commanded the highest prices; for example, when he and some other artists were commissioned to decorate the Château de Choisy in 1764, only Joseph Vernet was better paid. Such of his paintings as were sold by auction in his lifetime occasionally fetched large sums, though the prices paid at these sales varied a good deal. However, while he was considered as pre-eminent in his genre, this was thought to be a minor genre and not by any means on the same level as the high art of the painters of history and mythology. His style was recognized as perfect, as inimitable—but was it really painting? And although he is known to have been hostile to Chardin, Pierre—an influential man, who became Director of the Academy in 1770—was doubtlessly expressing a widespread opinion when he wrote the following to Chardin in 1778: "You must admit that, the work involved being equal, your compositions have never entailed such a costly outlay and considerable expenditure of time as those of your fellow artists practising the loftier types of art."

This sums the matter up, and explains why the artist received so few royal commissions and was practically ignored by Court circles. It also throws a favorable light on the discrimination of those art lovers who acquired his works—La Roque, an early friend of Watteau's, the one-legged man immortalized by the painter of the *Embarkation for Cythera*; Laurent de La Live de Jully; Charles Godefroy, the banker, portraits of whose two sons are now in the Louvre; Abbé Trublet and Abbé Pommyer. His works were also purchased by men of taste from countries other than France: Count Carl Gustav Tessin, who acquired a number of Chardin's masterpieces for Sweden; Prince Charles of Liechtenstein, who collected some of his most exquisite works (during the last few years these have made their way, one after the other, to Canada); and Dr William Hunter, the famous Glasgow physician and anatomist, who had the good sense to buy—and bequeath to his native city—three of Chardin's finest works, all dated 1738. In 1747, the *Mercure de France* commented: "It is annoying that various paintings by M. Chardin, such as *The Cistern, The Laundress,* and *The Morning Toilet,* should be taken abroad and lost to us."

One is struck, though hardly surprised, by the number of Chardin's pictures that figured in the collections and sales catalogues of other artists of his time—artists very different from him and from each other. We have already mentioned Jean-Baptiste Van Loo and Wille, but the list is much more long and varied: Aved, Jean-François de Troy, Hubert Robert, Dandré-Bardon, Taraval, Desfriches, the sculptors Caffieri, Lemoyne and in particular Pigalle (to whom Chardin paid tribute by depicting his *Mercury* in a number of his later works), engravers such as Laurent Cars and Le Bas, and goldsmiths such as Germain and Roettiers. Among the artists devoted to Chardin's works, the palm undoubtedly goes to Israel Silvestre's grandson, Nicolas Charles (1699-1767), "Drawing Master of the King's Children," who owned as many as sixteen of his pictures. These were put up for sale two years after the death of his son, Jacques-Augustin, in 1811, and were knocked down for only a few francs. The *Self-Portrait* and the *Portrait of Madame Chardin,* now among the glories of the Louvre, fetched only twenty-four francs between them.

Even in Chardin's lifetime, the sales value of his works— which had always tended to fluctuate in accordance with the state of the market and the changing tastes of collectors— began definitely to decline. Collectors of his work became increasingly few and far between, and this trend continued right up to the middle of the nineteenth century. The Louvre showed great daring in 1839, when it bought the two pastel *Self-Portraits* and the *Portrait of Madame Chardin* for 218 francs at the Bruzard sale.

Then, round about 1850, there was a general revival of interest in the eighteenth century. Writers and connoisseurs vied for the honor of having rediscovered Chardin. Several large

CLAY PIPE AND EARTHENWARE JUG, DETAIL. LOUVRE, PARIS.

collections in which his works occupied a place of honor were formed: the incomparable collection of Dr Louis La Caze, which came to the Louvre in 1869; François Marcille's collection, continued by his sons Camille and Eudoxe; the collection of the brothers Olympe and Ernest Lavalard, acquired by the Amiens museum in 1890; the collections of the Goncourt

CLAY PIPE AND EARTHENWARE JUG, DETAIL. LOUVRE, PARIS.

brothers, Laperlier (sold in 1867), Baron de Beurnonville, and Walferdin, and finally that of the *couturier* Doucet (sold in 1912). Chardin was appreciated again, the market value of his paintings soared, and further collections were formed: Leon Michel-Lévy's (sold in 1925), Daniel David-Weill's (now largely dispersed—the Edinburgh *Flower Piece* and the fine still life in Washington, *Two Rabbits and Pheasant*, both reproduced here, belonged to it), and above all that of Henri de Rothschild, which was begun in the nineteenth century by the Baroness Nathaniel de Rothschild and by 1931 contained no less than thirty-three paintings and a pastel by the artist.

The age of the great collections seems, however, to have passed. Only a few American museums are still in a position to acquire works by Chardin. Many fine items remain, jealously guarded and kept secret, in private hands, but during the last few years no Chardin of quality has come on the market without sooner or later entering a museum, generally a transatlantic one.

The revival of interest in Chardin among collectors went hand in hand with his rediscovery by the critics. In the eighteenth century, critical opinion had been far from unanimous on the merits of his work. Against the reservations expressed by Mariette and Lafont de Saint-Yenne can be set the opinions of Cochin and of Haillet de Couronne whose letters and memorial address are still fundamental to our knowledge of Chardin.

As for Diderot, his attitude is difficult to assess. He seemed to have shown little interest in the works by Chardin exhibited at Salons between 1759 and 1763. If he mentioned them at all, it was mainly to criticize. He placed the artist among the "slipshod painters." Then, at the Salon of 1763, his eyes were suddenly opened and he lavished praises on Chardin, devoting some of his finest writings to him. How can this change of mind be explained? We know—Diderot himself has indicated as much —that Chardin must have been a delightful conversationalist, even though he was incapable of expressing in the written word what he put into his works (very few of his writings have come down to us, and the best of them seem to have been dictated by Cochin). We also know that as the man responsible for hanging the pictures at the Salon, Chardin acted in the semi-official capacity of guide, providing Diderot with a commentary on the paintings shown. Diderot probably owed his discovery of Chardin's art to the painter himself, and was to go on praising it until the Salon of 1775, the last at which both men were present. Though deeply moved by Chardin's work, Diderot hardly succeeded in explaining its charm. True, much of what he had to say about it was admirable and perfectly apposite, and the descriptive passages are certainly excellent. But, while he was impressed by the miracle of Chardin's accomplishment, his approach was that of the man of letters rather than the critic; he expressed his enthusiasm without explaining it.

Round about 1780, the critics fell silent on the subject of Chardin's work. There were one or two exceptions—see, for example, the text by Le Carpentier quoted in the concluding chapter of this study—but, generally speaking, nobody seemed to be interested in him any more. Delacroix referred to him only incidentally, and Balzac related how a Chardin portrait of a woman was substituted for a Sebastiano del Piombo, at the expense of the unfortunate Cousin Pons. (Today, of course, that would not seem such a bad exchange.) Then, from about 1850, when collectors started to take an interest in his work, articles and scholarly studies on Chardin began to appear. An almost forgotten critic, Pierre Hédouin, can claim credit for the earliest serious study, published in 1856. He was followed by the Goncourt brothers, who played a major part in the rediscovery of Chardin. Although they tend to overstress certain social factors ("the bourgeois painter of the bourgeoisie"), their approach still strikes us as correct in tone and feeling.

Slowly and patiently, the catalogue of his works has been built up and perfected, thanks to Emmanuel Bocher (1876), Jean Guiffrey (1907), Herbert Furst (1911) and, in particular, the late Georges Wildenstein (1933). Articles and studies have abounded, including those of H. de Chennevières (1888), E. Pilon (1901), E. Schefer (1904), A. Dayot (1907), H. Pascal (Henri de Rothschild) and R. Gaucheron (1931), A. de Ridder (1932), and E. Goldschmidt (1945). Men of letters, from Théophile Gautier to Marcel Proust, from André Gide to André Malraux, have also been keenly interested in Chardin, and they have provided us with some of the most illuminating comments on his work.

Above all, however, Chardin is the painter's painter, one who has earned the most gratifying of tributes: the admiration of his peers. We have already seen how his colleagues paid him the honor of hanging his pictures on their walls, and a similar deference has been shown by later artists in their writings and, more particularly, in their paintings. Thus, the rediscovery of Chardin by collectors and painters was paralleled among artists by a whole post-Chardinesque movement, inspired in the main by his handling of paint. In the course of the nineteenth century, such French painters as Ribot (though he was even more strongly influenced by Ribera), Cals, Vollon, and above all Bonvin (see his *Servant drawing Water*, dated 1861, at the Louvre), Philippe Rousseau, Couture, and even Fantin-Latour echoed the technique of the eighteenth-century master (see the catalogue of the *Vier Franse Meesters* exhibition, Laren, 1962), though working in a rather heavier and darker medium. His most devoted imitator, however, was Decamps (1803-1860) who fumed at not being able to reproduce his colors: "Chardin's whites: I cannot hit on them!" The criticism of the time, rather to our surprise, placed the two artists on the same level, the Goncourts singling out Decamps as Chardin's most worthy heir.

A generation later, the critics compared Chardin's solid compositions with those of Cézanne. And, indeed, the painter of *The House of Cards* and the painter of *The Card-Players* are closely linked in spirit and approach.

Since then, Chardin has continued to grow in the esteem of other painters. Matisse copied *The Skate,* and the Cubists (Picasso and Juan Gris) were attracted by his arrangements of musical instruments (a genre that Baschenis had already handled with poetic feeling), while a picture like *Clay Pipe and Earthenware Jug* foreshadows the Braque of 1908 in its tranquillity and in the aesthetic pleasure afforded by its perfect composition. "Braque, as resolutely addicted to closed rooms as Chardin, opened no window in his paintings..." (Jean Leymarie). Nearer our own day Giorgio Morandi, that "metaphysical" painter of stark and stylized still lifes, has achieved something of the magical calm of the French master.

To each painter, in the terms of his own period, Chardin has something to give. His perfect construction could not have failed to impress Cézanne, his thick paintwork fascinated Van Gogh, while Braque was influenced by his solid craftsmanship and Matisse by his poetry.

And, indeed, in the last analysis Chardin's place may well be among the poet-painters with a concern for fine texture, between Vermeer (with whom the Goncourts already associated him) and Corot. In the present age of shock tactics and quick emotional effects in painting, there is surely a lesson to be learnt from these three painters of silence. All three make at least one demand in common—that you should pause at length in front of their works and watch a seemingly inanimate world come to life. And once your imagination has been caught by the fruit and glasses in a Chardin still life and lingers on them, these apparently ordinary things take on a new and unexpected significance, becoming a universe in themselves.

CHARDIN AND HIS CRITICS

When we read what has been written about Chardin from the eighteenth century to the present day, we are astonished by its incredible repetitiveness. The same anecdotes, the same judgments, the same words, the same turns of phrase recur again and again in an attempt to explain—while admitting that this is impossible—the inexplicable.

To avoid this repetitiveness we have ranged freely through the material available, without trying to illustrate any central argument. The quotations that follow are arranged chronologically and consist of old writings, extracts from more or less well-known criticisms, letters from painters, fragments from poems, and judgments by writers as well as critics.

This selection is not put forward in support of any thesis but in an attempt to lend fresh interest to a rather hackneyed subject.

SELF-PORTRAIT WITH AN EYESHADE. SIGNED AND DATED 1775. PASTEL.
LOUVRE, PARIS.

CHARDIN AND HIS CRITICS

R EMEMBER what Chardin said to us at the Salon:
"Gentlemen, gentlemen, may we crave your indulgence.
Look for the very worst among all these paintings; and then
remember that two thousand wretches have broken their paint
brushes between their teeth in despair at not being able to do
any better...

"After we have spent long days and nights studying motion-
less and inanimate objects, we are suddenly presented with the
living forms of nature; and all our years of work seem to come
to naught: we are as awkward as we were the first time we ever
lifted a pencil. We have to teach our eyes to look at nature; and
there are many who have never seen it, and never will. This is
the torment of our lives. We spend five or six years drawing
from models, and then we are left to fall back on our talent, if
we have any. And talent is not revealed at once. Its presence
or absence is not decided at the first attempt. And how many
attempts, both good and bad, we have to make...

"The painter who has never been aware of the difficulties of
art will never do anything worth while."

> Chardin as reported by Diderot in his review of the Salon
> of 1765.

His approach to painting is an individual one: there are no
finished lines, no smooth transitions; the brushwork is rough
and unpolished. It seems as if the paint has been pressed on to

CLAY PIPE AND EARTHENWARE JUG. SIGNED, UNDATED. LOUVRE, PARIS.

the canvas by the brush, and yet his figures are striking in their truthfulness, and his unusual approach seems to endow them with a greater naturalness and life.

> 1738, Chevalier de Neufville de Brunabois de Montador. Critical account of the pictures exhibited at the Louvre.

I would only point out that, taking it all in all, Monsieur Chardin's talent is no more than a renewal of that of the Le Nain brothers.

> 1749, Pierre-Jean Mariette, Abécédario.

His is a singular manner of painting. He applies his colors one after the other, so that his picture resembles a kind of patchwork, like a tapestry made with the *point carré* stitch.

> 1750, Abbé Raynal, Correspondence.

Chardin is an intelligent man; he understands the theory of his art; he paints in a manner entirely his own, and his paintings will be sought after one day. He handles his small figures as generously as if they were cubits tall.

> 1759, Diderot, Salon.

He always gives us a very faithful rendering of nature, and has his own individual technique; his execution is rough, almost harsh; his subjects are everyday domestic ones. For some time the painter has finished nothing; he no longer takes the trouble to do the hands or the feet. He works like a man of the world who has talent and facility and is satisfied to outline his ideas with a few strokes of the brush. He has now put himself in the forefront of the slipshod painters, after having done a great many things that entitled him to a place among artists of the first rank.

> 1761, Diderot, Salon.

Here you come, Chardin, just in time to restore my sight which your fellow-artist Challe has so sorely afflicted. Here you are again, you great magician, with your silent compositions! How eloquently they speak to the artist! How much they have to say about the imitation of nature and the science of color and harmony How the air circulates among these objects, and sunlight itself does not better reduce the disparities between the things it falls upon. For you there are neither matching nor clashing colors. . . . No verve; little genius; hardly any poetry; a great deal of technique and truth; and that's all.

1765, Diderot, Salon.

It is said of him that he has a unique technique, and that he uses his thumb as much as his brush. I don't know what truth there is in that... Whatever his method, his paintings appeal to the uncultured and the connoisseur alike. They display incredible strength of color, over-all harmony, incisiveness and truth, admirable mass effects, a magic of execution that can drive you to despair, a piquancy of pattern and lay-out. Stand back, go up close, and you will have the same impression, no confusion, yet no symmetry either, because there is calm and rest. You halt in front of a Chardin instinctively, just as the weary traveler will sit down, almost without noticing it, in a spot that offers him greenery, silence, shade, and water.

1767, Diderot, Salon.

Chardin is such a vigorous imitator of nature and such a severe self-critic that I have seen a still life of game that he left unfinished because the young rabbits he had been using as models had gone bad, and he felt that he could not achieve the harmony he had in mind with any others. All those that were brought to him were either too dark or too light in color.

1769, Diderot, Salon.

Here is Diderot's only comment on the pastels, including the Self-Portrait *reproduced here, which Chardin exhibited for the first time at the Salon of 1771:*

Three studies of heads in pastel. Here, as always, we have the same sure, free hand, the same eyes used to seeing nature, but to seeing it well and drawing out the magic of its effects.

1771, Diderot, Salon.

Of all the painters of our time, M. Chardin was perhaps the most gifted in the use of color. His feeling for it was unfailingly exquisite, and his eyes seemed to be like prisms capable of breaking down each object into its component tones, distinguishing the subtlest of transitions between light and shade. No one had a better knowledge of the magic of chiaroscuro.

When he spoke of it, one word was enough to demonstrate the piercing quality of his eye, its sense of harmony. He paid no heed to the conventions of his craft, or rather he was not aware of them.

1780, Renou, Memorial Address on Chardin.

Speaking of Chardin's youth:

M. Chardin believed at that time that he must compose everything out of his head, and that reliance on nature betokened a lack of talent.

He felt that he should not consider depicting every hair (on a rabbit) or render it in too great detail. "Here is an object to be painted," he would say to himself. "To achieve a truthful rendering of it, I must forget everything I have seen and even the way in which such objects have been treated by others. I must place it sufficiently far away not to be able to see the details. I must apply myself to copying, with the greatest verisimilitude, the general masses, the shades of color, the curves, the effects of light and shadow."

He spent a great deal of time over each picture.

...He painted them over and over until he had achieved that breaking down of tones produced by the distance of the object and the reflections of all the surrounding objects.

...One day an artist was going on at length about all he did to purify and perfect his colors. M. Chardin, annoyed at hearing such talk from a man whom he knew to be no more than a cold and careful technician, said to him: "But who told you that painting was done with colors?" "What is it done with, then?" the other artist asked in surprise. "Colors are employed," said M. Chardin, "but painting is done with emotions."

1780, Letters from Cochin giving Haillet de Couronne, Secretary of the Academy of Rouen, material for a memorial address on Chardin.

It would be a good idea to place a picture by Chardin in every studio as a demonstration of true harmony and color sense in painting, indeed, as a complete text-book of effects, harmony, chiaroscuro, and color.

1821, C. Le Carpentier, Galerie des peintres célèbres.

The difference between Chardin's talent and Oudry's is that every decoration by Chardin is a true and solid painting, whereas every painting by Oudry is a skillful decoration.

1860, W. Bürger (Thoré), Exposition de tableaux de l'Ecole française ancienne, Gazette des Beaux-Arts.

Against one of those blurred, muted backgrounds that he does so well, where a cavern coolness mingles vaguely with a sideboard gloom, or on one of those typical tables of his with their mossy tones and dull marble, Chardin has set out the plates for a dessert. Here are the downy velvet of the peach, the amber transparency of the white grape, the sugar frosting of the plum,

THE SKATE. LOUVRE, PARIS.

the damp crimson of the strawberries, the thick grain of the muscat and its bluish bloom, the wrinkles and warts on the orange peel, the lacy embroidery of the melons, the blotches on the old apples, the knots in the breadcrust, the smooth shell of the chestnut, even the woody texture of the hazelnut. They are all there in front of you, in the light and air of day, and it seems as though you could reach out and touch them. With its

THE SKATE, DETAIL. LOUVRE, PARIS.

appetizing color, downy skin and pulpy flesh, each fruit looks as though it had fallen straight from the tree on to the canvas.

...Chardin paints everything he sees.

No subject is too humble for his brush. Here is the larder of the populace, the old cauldron, the pepper-pot, the wooden mortar with its pestle, the lowliest pieces of furniture. There is no aspect of nature that he despises.

...The miracle in Chardin's paintings is this: modeled in their own mass and shape, drawn with their own light, created so to speak from the soul of their color, the objects seem to detach themselves from the canvas and become alive, by some wonderful optical illusion operating in space between the canvas and the onlooker.

> 1863-1864, Edmond and Jules de Goncourt, Gazette des Beaux-Arts.

There is a sort of honesty in the air breathed by these people, in the furniture they choose, in the clothes and colors they wear, in the processes of their daily life.

> 1877, Philippe Burty, Maîtres et petits maîtres.

Chardin began with "natures mortes," the term used for inanimate objects, for in reality nothing in nature is dead. In exactness of imitation, force of color, solidity of paint, he can be set beside the Flemish and Dutch masters. Working in this pleasantly affected and agreeably artificial genre, he yet achieves the absolute truth; he is a realist in the best sense of the word.

> 1882, Théophile Gautier, Guide de l'Amateur au Musée du Louvre, suivi de la vie et des œuvres de quelques peintres.

But Chardin!

I have often wished to know something about Chardin the man.

His bonhomie, like Corot's, was that of the common people, but he had more disappointments, more dreams in his life.

I very much liked what he (Goncourt) said about Chardin. I am more and more convinced that true painters do not "finish" their pictures, in the sense too often applied to the word, that

THE ATTRIBUTES OF MUSIC, DETAIL. SIGNED AND DATED 1765.
LOUVRE, PARIS.

THE SKATE, DETAIL. LOUVRE, PARIS.

is, with everything so meticulous you could stick your nose into it. When you look at them closely, the best—and indeed the most technically complete—pictures are seen to be made up of strokes of color placed closely together. They do not make their effect until you stand a certain distance away from them... From this point of view Chardin is as great as Rembrandt.

...There are so many things I should like to tell you, particularly as Chardin has given me so much to think about, notably on the subject of color and the importance of not resorting to local color. I find the following remark magnificent: "How can we pin down, how can we say, what has gone to make that toothless mouth, with its infinitely delicate touches? It was made simply with a few traces of 'yellow' and some streaks of 'blue'." When I read that, I thought of the view of the town by Vermeer of Delft at the Hague.

1885, Vincent van Gogh, Letter to his brother Theo.

This response of tone to tone, this interplay of the smallest touches of color, repeated as though at random and resembling notes in harmony, this constant music made up of crisscrossing echoes, always discreet, but always there, the sense of a delicate understructure, the skillful setting-off of one light effect by another.

1889, H. de Chennevières, Chardin au Musée du Louvre, Gazette des Beaux-Arts.

Go to the gallery of pastels and see Chardin's self-portrait, which he made when he was seventy. The huge spectacles are perched on the end of his nose, pinching it between their two brand-new disks of glass, and above them the dim pupils of his failing eyes look upwards with an air of having seen much, twinkled much, and loved much. They seem to be saying half-boastfully, half-wistfully: "Yes, indeed, I'm an old man now."

THE ATTRIBUTES OF MUSIC. SIGNED AND DATED 1765.
LOUVRE, PARIS (OVERDOOR PANEL FROM THE CHATEAU DE CHOISY).

Though softened and subdued by age, they have not lost all their glow, but the tired eyelids—like clasps worn down with use—are red-rimmed. Like the old coat he has thrown round his body, his skin has become stiff and faded. The pink tints of the flesh, like those of the material, are still undimmed, indeed almost heightened, and here and there the skin has taken on a golden, pearly sheen. The worn colors of the one echo those of the other, being the colors of all things as they approach their end—dying embers, decaying leaves, setting suns, clothes that are cast aside, and men who pass away—, infinitely delicate, rich, and gentle. How admirably and exactly the fold of the mouth and the crease in the nose answer to the set of the eye. The slightest fold in the skin, the slightest molding of a vein, is an exact and meticulous rendering of three corresponding features of the original: character, life, and feeling.

Chardin's slovenliness in the other pastel self-portrait he has left us is laughably reminiscent of the strange costume of some elderly English tourist. From the eyeshade vigorously pulled down over the forehead to the scarf knotted round the neck, every detail of the formidable and negligent attire in which he has arrayed himself for the night seems as much an indication of taste as one of a fine contempt for the niceties of dress. If the pink neckcloth is so old, that is because old pinks are softer. When we see those pink and yellow knots reflected in the pinks and yellows of the skin and the dark glint of the spectacles reflected by the blue rim of the eyeshade, our initial astonishment at the old man's outlandish garb melts before its gentle charm, and we experience pleasure of the highest kind at finding, in the apparent disarray of this old bourgeois in his nightclothes, the noble hierarchy of precious colors, an order imposed by the laws of beauty.

About 1895, Marcel Proust, Portraits de Peintres ("Contre Sainte-Beuve," 1954).

Do you remember that fine pastel of Chardin in spectacles with an eyeshade jutting out above them? This painter was cunning as a fox. Have you ever noticed how, by means of light transversal lines across the nose, he brings his values into clearer focus? Check this, and see if I am mistaken.

1904, Letter from Cézanne to Emile Bernard.

Unlike Watteau, the master of gesture, he attains perfection only in the portrayal of immobility.

...His power of imitation, that illusionist skill praised by all his contemporaries, is among the least of this extraordinary painter's merits. If that were all, Chardin would hardly rise above the level of Desportes. He is much more than an imitator of nature. Even in the most ordinary objects, the form is always monumentally conceived. A magnificence—where it comes from, I don't know—imbues his subjects without changing them or disturbing their silence. It is a radiance of the heart, an emotion that blends with nature and endows it with the painter's own power and compassion.

1929, Louis Gillet, La peinture au Musée du Louvre, Ecole française, XVIIIe siècle.

The object is neither a picturesque motif nor the excuse for a pleasant exercise or a pretty arabesque. It exists in its own right and *per se*. Chardin recognizes that it has its own personality and takes its *raison d'être* into account. Hence the attention he pays to the features peculiar to the object and the care with which he suggests its essence.

1949, F. Jourdain, Chardin.

But some masters really seem to have surrendered themselves to the humblest of subjects, and have claimed that this submission helped to develop their talent. Such artists often belong to a special type of human being, the Chardins, the Corots; and they are the least romantic men imaginable... But Chardin's seeming humility involved not so much submission to the model as its covert destruction in the interests of his picture. He used to say that "one paints with emotions, not with colors"; but with his emotions he created peaches. The boy in *The Draftsman* has no more emotional appeal than the still life with a pitcher, and the splendid blue of the carpet on which he is playing hardly keeps within the bounds of realism. The housewife in the *Return from Market* is a first-class Braque, dressed up just enough to deceive the onlooker... Chardin is not just an eighteenth-century little master, more sensitive than his rivals; he is, like Corot, a discreet but imperious simplifier. His quiet mastery destroyed the baroque still life of the Dutch school, showed up his contemporaries as mere decorators, and from Watteau's death to the Revolution there was no one to be compared with him in France...

1951, André Malraux, The Voices of Silence.

Chardin does not withdraw to a world of gods
or heroes of religion or the old mythologies.
  When the old myths mean nothing more
to us, *felix culpa!* we begin to believe
in everyday reality.
  I think we shall more and more
give thanks to artists who, by silence,
by simply ignoring themes imposed by
the ideology of the day, prove their communion
with the non-artists of their time.
  Because they have been one with the truly living
background of the time, with its unofficial state of mind,
ignoring its ideological superstructures.

1963, Francis Ponge, Art de France, III.

THE ATTRIBUTES OF MUSIC, DETAIL. SIGNED AND DATED 1765.
LOUVRE, PARIS.

BIBLIOGRAPHY
GENERAL INDEX
LIST OF COLOR PLATES
TABLE OF CONTENTS

SELECT BIBLIOGRAPHY

The standard work on Chardin is the monograph by Georges Wildenstein, published in 1933 by Editions d'Etudes et de Documents (Beaux-Arts), Paris. A new, revised edition of this work is to be published by the Phaidon Press, London, in both French and English, towards the end of 1963. The 1933 edition contains an exhaustive bibliography (pp. 251-257).

Here, for the period prior to 1933, we include only a selection of the most important works, listed in alphabetical order. For the period since 1933, however, we have compiled a more detailed bibliography, though we cannot claim to have included everything that has been written about Chardin; works in this section are listed in the order of publication.

BEFORE 1933
Authors listed in alphabetical order

1. Source Works

L. P. DE BACHAUMONT, *Mémoires secrets* (supposed to be by Bachaumont), 36 vols., London 1784-1789. — BAILLET DE SAINT-JULIEN, *Lettre à M. Ch(ardin) sur les caractères en peinture*, Geneva 1753. — BAILLET DE SAINT-JULIEN, *Réflexions sur quelques circonstances présentes contenant deux lettres sur l'exposition des tableaux au Louvre cette année 1748*, 1748. — C. N. COCHIN, *Lettres de Charles-Nicolas Cochin à Haillet de Couronne*, first published by Charles de Beaurepaire in *Documents sur Chardin*, *Précis analytique de l'Académie des Sciences... de Rouen*, 1875-1876. — C. N. COCHIN, *Lettre à un amateur en réponse aux critiques qui ont paru sur l'exposition des tableaux*, 1753. — D. DIDEROT, *Œuvres complètes*, edited by J. Assézat, 20 vols., Paris 1875-1877. — F. ENGERAND, *Inventaire des collections de la couronne. Inventaire des tableaux commandés et achetés par la Direction des Bâtiments du Roi, 1709-1729*, Paris 1900. — M. FURCY-RAYNAUD, *Chardin et M. d'Angivillers, correspondance inédite*, Paris 1900. — Abbé L. GOUGENOT, *Lettre sur la peinture, sculpture et architecture*, Paris 1748. — J. B. G. HAILLET DE COURONNE, *Eloge de Chardin*, read before the Academy of Rouen in 1780, published in *Mémoires inédits*, edited by E. Dussieux, Soulié, Chennevières, etc., Vol. II, Paris 1854. — LAFONT DE SAINT-YENNE, *Réflexions sur quelques causes de l'état présent de la peinture en France*, Paris 1747. — C. LE CARPENTIER, *Galerie des peintres célèbres*, 2 vols., Paris 1821. — C. J. MATHON DE LA COUR,

Lettres à M.*** sur les peintures, les sculptures et les gravures exposées au Salon du Louvre en 1765, Paris 1765. — P. J. MARIETTE, *Abécédario*, edited by Chennevières, Montaiglon, etc., Archives de l'Art français, 1851-1862, 6 vols. (the *Notice sur Chardin* in the *Abécédario* is dated 1749). — A. DE MONTAIGLON, *Procès-Verbaux de l'Académie royale de Peinture et de Sculpture, 1648-1793*, edited by Montaiglon, 1875-1892, 11 vols. — Chevalier de NEUFVILLE DE BRUNAUBOIS-MONTADOR, *Description raisonnée des tableaux exposés au Louvre*, Paris 1738. — M. TOURNEUX, *Correspondance littéraire, philosophique et critique de Grimm, Diderot, Raynal*, edited by Tourneux, 16 vols., Paris 1877-1882. — J. G. WILLE, *Mémoires et Journal*, edited by Duplessis, 2 vols., Paris 1857.

2. *General Works on the 18th Century*

C. BLANC, *Histoire des peintres de toutes les écoles. Ecole française*, 3 vols., Paris 1865. — A. DAYOT, *La peinture française au XVIIIe siècle*, 3 vols., Paris n.d. — L. DIMIER, *Les peintres français du XVIIIe siècle*, 2 vols., Paris-Brussels 1928-1930. — L. DUMONT-WILDEN, *Le portrait en France*, Brussels 1909. — A. FONTAINE, *Les doctrines d'art en France, peintres, amateurs, critiques, de Poussin à Diderot*, Paris 1909. — L. GILLET, *La peinture au musée du Louvre. Ecole française, XVIIIe siècle*, L'Illustration, Paris n.d. (1929). — E. and J. DE GONCOURT, *L'Art au XVIIIe siècle*, 2nd edition, Paris 1873 (many editions, that of 1906 being the one most generally referred to); English edition, *French XVIII Century Painters*, translated by Robin Ironside, London 1948. — L. GONSE, *Les chefs-d'œuvre des musées de province*, Paris 1900. — J. LOCQUIN, *La peinture d'histoire en France de 1747 à 1785*, Paris 1912. — P. MARCEL, *La peinture française au début du XVIIIe siècle, 1690-1721*, Paris 1906. — P. RATOUIS DE LIMAY and E. DACIER, *Les pastels français du XVIIe et du XVIIIe siècle*, Paris-Brussels 1927. — L. REAU, *Histoire de la peinture française au XVIIIe siècle*, 2 vols., Paris 1925.

3. *Monographs and Important Articles*

E. BOCHER, *La gravure française au XVIIIe siècle ou catalogue raisonné des estampes, pièces en couleur, au bistre et au lavis de 1700 à 1800*, 6 parts, 1875-1882 (Part III, *Chardin*, published in 1876). — C.P. DE CHENNEVIÈRES, *Portraits inédits d'artistes français*, Paris 1853. — H. DE CHENNEVIÈRES, *Chardin au Musée du Louvre (la donation Lacaze)*, Gazette des Beaux-Arts, 1888-1889, 2 articles. — CORNU, *Chardin*, in Thieme-Becker, Vol. VI, 1912, p. 388. — A. DAYOT, *J. B. Siméon Chardin, 1699-1779*, with a catalogue by J. Guiffrey, Paris n.d. — A. DAYOT and L. VAILLAT, *L'œuvre de J. B. Siméon Chardin et de J. H. Fragonard*, Paris 1907. — E. DILKE, *Chardin et ses œuvres à Potsdam et à Stockholm*, Gazette des Beaux-Arts, 1899. —

L. DE FOURCAUD, *J. B. Siméon Chardin*, Paris 1900 (Bibliothèque de l'art ancien et moderne). — H. FURST, *Chardin*, London 1911. — E. and J. DE GONCOURT, *Chardin*, Gazette des Beaux-Arts, 1863-1864. — O. GRAUTOFF, *Chardin*, Kunst und Künstler, 1908. — J. GUIFFREY, *Catalogue raisonné de l'œuvre peint et dessiné de Jean-Baptiste Siméon Chardin*, Paris 1908. — P. HÉDOUIN, *Mosaïque: peintres, musiciens, artistes dramatiques*, Paris 1856. — V. JOSZ, *Les graveurs de Chardin*, Mercure de France, 1907. — T. KLINGSOR, *Chardin*, Collection Maîtres anciens et modernes, Paris 1924. — C. NORMAND, *Jean-Baptiste Siméon Chardin*, Collection Les artistes célèbres, Paris 1901. — A. PASCAL and R. GAUCHERON, *Documents sur la vie et l'œuvre de Chardin*, Paris 1931 (including a catalogue of the pictures in the Henri de Rothschild Collection and a list of articles on the 1929 Chardin exhibition). — E. PILON, *Chardin*, Paris n.d. (1909). — A. DE RIDDER, *Jean-Baptiste Siméon Chardin*, Paris 1932. — E. SCHEFER, *Chardin*, Paris 1904.

4. Exhibitions

1907, Paris, Galerie Georges Petit, *Chardin-Fragonard*. — 1926, New York, Wildenstein Gallery, *Chardin*. — 1929, Paris, Galerie Pigalle, *L'œuvre de Jean-Baptiste Siméon Chardin*.

AFTER 1933
Works listed in chronological order

1. General Works on the 18th Century

A. LEROY, *La peinture française au XVIIIᵉ siècle*, Paris 1934. — P. JAMOT, *La peinture en France*, Paris 1934. — L. GILLET, *La peinture française de Poussin à David*, Manuels d'histoire de l'art, Paris 1935. — W. PINDER, *Gesammelte Aufsätze aus den Jahren 1907-1935*, edited by L. Bruhns, Leipzig 1938, pp. 31-38. — L. HOURTICQ, *La peinture française au XVIIIᵉ siècle*, Paris 1939. — S. ROCHEBLAVE, *La peinture française au XVIIIᵉ siècle*, 1937. — T. GOSSELIN (LE NOTRE), *Existences d'artistes français (Greuze, Fragonard, Chardin, Hubert Robert)*, Paris 1940. — Vicomte C. DU PELOUX, *Répertoire biographique et bibliographique des artistes du XVIIIᵉ siècle français*, Vol. II, Paris 1941 (Vol. I published in 1930). — B. DORIVAL, *La peinture française*, 2 vols., Paris 1942. — P. RATOUIS DE LIMAY, *Le pastel en France au XVIIIᵉ siècle*, Paris 1946. — M. FLORISOONE, *Le XVIIIᵉ siècle*, Paris 1948. — P. LAVALLÉE, *Le dessin français*, Paris 1948. — E. DACIER and L. RÉAU, *L'art au XVIIIᵉ siècle en France*, Nouvelles Encyclopédies illustrées, Vol. II, Paris 1951-1952. — F. BOUCHER and P. JACCOTTET, *Le dessin français au XVIIIᵉ siècle*, Lausanne 1952. — C. STERLING, *La nature morte de l'antiquité à nos jours*, Paris 1952; new, revised edition, Paris 1959;

in English, *Still Life Painting from Antiquity to the Present Day*, New York and London 1959. — G. BAZIN, *Trésors de la peinture au musée du Louvre*, Paris 1957. — C. STERLING, *Musée de l'Ermitage: la peinture française de Poussin à nos jours*, Paris 1957. — J. CHARPIER and P. SEGHERS, *L'art de la peinture*, Paris 1957. — J. SEZNEC and J. ADHÉMAR, *Diderot Salons*, Vol. I (Salons 1759-1761-1763), Oxford 1957; Vol. II (Salon 1765), Oxford 1960; Vol. III (Salon 1767), Oxford 1963. — R. HUYGHE, *La peinture française du XVIIe et du XVIIIe siècle*, Paris 1962. — J. VERGNET-RUIZ and M. LACLOTTE, *Petits et grands musées de France: La peinture française des primitifs à nos jours*, Paris 1962. — A. CHATELET and J. THUILLIER, *French Painting, From Le Nain to Fragonard*, Geneva (in preparation, to be published 1964).

2. *Monographs*

M. FLORISOONE, *Chardin*, Trésors de la Peinture française, Geneva 1938. — E. PILON, *Chardin*, Paris 1941. — E. GOLDSCHMIDT, *Chardin*, Stockholm 1945. — F. JOURDAIN, *Chardin*, Collection Les Maîtres, Paris 1949. — B. DENVIS, *Chardin*, Paris 1950 (also published in English). — DONAT DE CHAPEAUROUGE, *Die Stilleben Chardins in der Karlsruher Galerie*, Karlsruhe 1955. — SOLOTOV, *Jean-Baptiste Siméon Chardin*, Moscow 1955. — J. S. NEMILOVA, *J. Siméon Chardin et ses tableaux au Musée national de l'Ermitage*, Leningrad 1961.

3. *Important Articles*

J. BABELON, *J.B.S. Chardin*, Beaux-Arts, No. 50, 1933, pp. 1 and 8 (excellent review of Wildenstein's monograph). — M. A. BANKS, *A Still Life by Chardin*, Bulletin of the Rhode Island School of Design, Providence 1933, pp. 52-55. — J. MATHEY, *Jeaurat, Cochin, Durameau et les dessins de Chardin*, Bulletin de la Société de l'Histoire de l'Art français, 1933, pp. 82-86. — J. MATHEY, *Etienne Jeaurat*, Old Master Drawings, Vol. VIII, 1933, pp. 8-10. — G. WILDENSTEIN, *Le caractère de Chardin et sa vie*, Gazette des Beaux-Arts, II, 1933, pp. 365-380 (extract from the monograph). — E. FRANCIS, *Chardin and his Engravers*, The Print Collectors' Quarterly, 1934-1935, pp. 229-249. — M. R. R., *The Silver Goblet by J. B. S. Chardin*, Bulletin of the City Art Museum of St Louis, 1935, pp. 52-55. — H. ROSTRUP, *Fra Chardin til Greuze*, Vol. II, Tilskunen, 1935, pp. 267-285. — A. ROSTAND, *J. B. Descamps*, 1715-1791, Bulletin de la Société des Antiquaires de Normandie, 1936, pp. 271-290. — G. WILDENSTEIN, *Premier supplément à la biographie et au catalogue de J. A. J. Aved* (1922-1935), Gazette des Beaux-Arts, I, 1936, pp. 159-172. — H. NOTTHAFFT, *" Les attributs des arts " de Chardin au Musée de l'Ermitage*, Annuaire du Musée de l'Ermitage à Léningrad, Vol. II, 1937, pp. 1-18. — J. ROBIQUET, *Notice sur les "brouettes"*, *"roulettes"* ou *"vinaigrettes"*. *A propos d'un dessin de Chardin au Musée National de Stockholm*, Nationalmusei arsbok, VIII, 1938, pp. 130-132. T. ROUSSEAU, Jr., *A Pastel Portrait by Jean-Baptiste Siméon Chardin*, Bulletin of the Fogg Museum of Art, 1940, pp. 42-44. — E. PILON, *Chardin rue Princesse et aux Galeries du Louvre*, Visages du Monde, No. 74, July 1941, pp. 18-20. — F. SWEET, *The White Table-cloth by Chardin*, Bulletin of The Art Institute of Chicago, Vol. 39, 1945, pp. 50-53. — O. BENESCH, *Two Drawings dedicated to Madame de Pompadour*, Gazette des Beaux-Arts, I, 1950, pp. 125-129 and 175-176. — T. ROUSSEAU, Jr., *A Boy Blowing Bubbles by Chardin*, The Metropolitan Museum of Art Bulletin, April 1950, pp. 221-227. — E. S. H., *A Painting by Chardin in the Jacobs Collection*, News: The Baltimore Museum of Art, Vol. XIV, No. 5, 1950-1951, pp. 1-4. — K. MARTIN, *Notes on a Still Life by Chardin*, Allen Memorial Art Museum Bulletin (Oberlin College), Vol. 9, 1951, pp. 17-23. — R.S.D., *Institute purchases a Great Still Life by Chardin*, The Minneapolis Institute of Art Bulletin, October 1954, pp. 49-51. — A. MORGAN, *Chardin and French 18th Century Painting*, The Minneapolis Institute of Art Bulletin, October 1954, pp. 52-55. — M. PROUST, *Chardin, The Essence of Things*, Art News, October 1954, pp. 38-42 and 72-73 (English translation of the pages on Chardin in *Contre Sainte-Beuve* by Marcel Proust). — N. WALLIS, *Chardin, The Superlative Craftsman*, The Connoisseur, Vol. 133, April 1954, p. 111. — A. P. DE MIRIMONDE, *Musée de Besançon. De Chardin à Potke Verhagen*, Revue des Arts, 1955, pp. 185-187. — C. STERLING, *A Catalogue of French Painting, Metropolitan Museum of Art, New York*, Cambridge 1955, pp. 125-130. — L. EINSTEIN, *Looking at French 18th Century Pictures of The National Gallery in Washington*, Gazette des Beaux-Arts, May 1956, pp. 232-235. — M. DAVIES, *National Gallery Catalogues: French School*, 1957, 2nd edition, pp. 28-30. — K. MARTIN, *Bemerkungen zu zwei Kopien nach Stilleben von Jean-Baptiste Siméon Chardin*, in Festschrift Kurt Bauch, 1957, pp. 238-244. — J. RUSSELL, *Un médecin collectionneur au XVIIIe siècle*, L'Œil, No. 31-32, Summer 1957, pp. 12-19. — E. TURNER, *La serinette by Jean-Baptiste Chardin, A Study in Patronage and Technique*, Gazette des Beaux-Arts, I, 1957, pp. 299-310. — J. WILHELM, *Peinture et publicité*, L'Œil, No. 37, January 1958, pp. 50-53. — H. ADHÉMAR, *Une nature morte de Michel-Honoré Bounieu autrefois attribuée à Chardin*, Bulletin du Laboratoire du Musée du Louvre, 1959, pp. 63-66. — J. BARRELET, *Chardin du point de vue de la verrerie*, Gazette des Beaux-Arts, I, 1959, pp. 305-314. — E. and J. GONCOURT, *Chardin peintre de la bourgeoisie*, Jardin des Arts, January 1959, pp. 156-162 (reprinted from *L'Art au XVIIIe siècle*). — P. HUISMAN, *La collection Marcille: 5000 tableaux méconnus*, Connaissance des Arts, No. 88, June 1959, pp. 74-81. — G. WILDENSTEIN, *A propos de la jeunesse et des débuts de Chardin*, Nouvelles Archives de l'Art français, 1959, pp. 175-178. — G. WILDENSTEIN, *Le décor de la vie de Chardin d'après ses tableaux*, Gazette des Beaux-Arts, I, 1959, pp. 97-106. — H. ADHÉMAR, *Chardin*, in Enciclopedia Universale dell'Arte, Vol. III, 1960, pp. 454-459. — C.

EISLER, *A Chardin in the Grand Manner*, The Metropolitan Museum of Art Bulletin, February 1960, pp. 202-212. — U. CHRISTOFFEL, *Vom Stilleben Zurbaran und Chardin*, in Eberhard Hanfstaengh: Zum 75. Geburtstag, 1961, pp. 52-58. — P. GRATE, *Largillierre et les natures mortes de Grenoble*, La Revue du Louvre, 1961, pp. 30. — R. C. SAISSELIN, *Ut pictura poesis, Dubos to Diderot*, Journal of Aesthetic Art and Criticism, Winter 1961, p. 154. — F. PONGE, *De la nature morte de Chardin*, Art de France, 1963, pp. 253-264.

4. Major Exhibitions

1935, Copenhagen, Charlottenborg Palace, *L'art français au XVIIIᵉ siècle*. — 1937, Paris, Palais National des Arts, *Chefs-d'œuvre de l'art français*. — 1949, Geneva, Musée Rath, *Trois siècles de peinture française*. — 1952, Paris, Orangerie, *La nature morte, de l'antiquité à nos jours*. — 1954-1955, London, Royal Academy, *European Masters of the 18th Century*. — 1956, Paris, G.B.A., *De Watteau à Prudhon*. — 1957-1958, Paris, Orangerie, *Le portrait français de Watteau à David*. — 1958, Munich, Residenz, *Europäisches Rokoko*. — 1958, Stockholm, Nationalmuseum, *Fem sekler Fransk Konst*. — 1958, Bordeaux, *Paris et les ateliers provinciaux au XVIIIᵉ siècle*. — 1959, Paris, Galerie Heim, *Hommage à Chardin*.

GENERAL INDEX

Amiens, Musée de Picardie 26, 72, 75, 85.
Amigoni Jacopo (1682?-1752) 12.
Angers, Musée des Beaux-Arts 14, 39, 71.
Angiviller Comte d', Director General of Royal Buildings (1774-1791) 15, 16, 24.
Année Littéraire (L') 15.
Antwerp 26.
Aubry Etienne d' (1745-1781) 79.
Aved Jacques-André Joseph (1702-1766) 11, 22, 30/33, 83.

Bachelier Jean-Jacques (1724-1805) 79.
Balzac Honoré de (1799-1850) 87.
Baschenis Evaristo (1607/1617-1677) 89.
Bazin Germain 75.
Bellevue, Château de 14, 37.
Berlin, Staatliche Museen, Gemälde-galerie 8, 9, 44, 45, 50; Staatliche Schlösser und Gärten 27, 45.
Beurnonville, Collection of the Baron de 86.
Bocher Emmanuel, Chardin Catalogue (1876) 88.
Bonvin F. Léon (1834-1866) 88.
Boucher François (1703-1770) 5, 7, 15, 31, 78.
Bounieu Michel-Honoré (1740-1814) 79.

Braque Georges (1882-1963) 6, 60, 89, 108.
Bruzard Sale (1839) 84.
Bürger W. (Théophile Thoré) 98.
Burty Philippe 101.

Caffieri Jean-Jacques (1725-1792) 83.
Cals Adolf Franz (1810-1880) 88.
Carcassonne, Musée des Beaux-Arts 12.
Cars Laurent (1702-1771) 12, 83.
Cazes Pierre-Jacques (1676-1754) 8, 19/22.
Cézanne Paul (1839-1906) 6, 43, 89, 107.
Challe (active 1765-1772) 96.
Chardin Jean-Siméon (1699-1779), works mentioned:
Amiens, Musée de Picardie: *Two Wild Rabbits,* or *Return from the Hunt* 72, 75;
Angers, Musée des Beaux-Arts: *Basket of Grapes* 14, 71; *Peach, Plums, Biscuits, etc. on a Table* 39;
Berlin, Schlösser und Gärten: *Lady sealing a Letter* (1733) 9, 27, 30, 45;
Berlin, Staatliche Museen: *The Draftsman* (1737) 10, 44, 45, 50, 108;
Carcassonne, Musée des Beaux-Arts: *Makings of a Lunch* (1756) 12;
Edinburgh, National Gallery: *Flower Piece* 13, 70, 75;

LIST OF COLOR PLATES

CONTENTS

THIS, THE FORTIETH VOLUME OF "THE TASTE OF OUR TIME"
SERIES, WAS PRODUCED BY THE TECHNICAL STAFF OF EDITIONS
D'ART ALBERT SKIRA. FINISHED THE TWENTY-FIFTH DAY
OF SEPTEMBER, NINETEEN HUNDRED AND SIXTY-THREE.

TEXT AND ILLUSTRATIONS PRINTED BY

COLOR STUDIOS

IMPRIMERIES RÉUNIES S.A., LAUSANNE

PLATES ENGRAVED BY GUEZELLE & RENOUARD, PARIS

PHOTOGRAPHS BY

*Maurice Babey, Basel (pages 3, 18, 36, 38, 39, 42, 49, 56, 57, 59, 61, 62, 64, 66,
71, 72, 84, 85, 94, 102, 105, 109), Henry B. Beville, Washington (pages 41, 73,
80), Louis Laniepce, Paris (pages 63, 69, 99, 100, 103), Walter Steinkopf, Berlin
(page 44), Tom Scott, Edinburgh (page 70), Scala, Florence (page 48), and the
photographic services of the University of Glasgow (pages 28, 32, 52, 53, 54, 55)
and of the Nationalmuseum, Stockholm (pages 47, 58, 74, 76).*

PRINTED IN SWITZERLAND